C·A·K·E
Decorating

FAY GARDNER'S

C·A·K·E Decorating

ANGUS
& ROBERTSON
PUBLISHERS

ANGUS & ROBERTSON PUBLISHERS

Unit 4, Eden Park, 31 Waterloo Road,
North Ryde, NSW, Australia 2113, and
16 Golden Square, London W1R 4BN,
United Kingdom

First published in Australia
by Angus & Robertson Publishers in 1988
Published by arrangement with
Bacragas Pty. Ltd.

Copyright © Fay Gardner

ISBN 0 207 15884 3.

Design by Willy Richards
Photography by David Liddle
Typeset in 12pt Elante
by The Type Shop Pty. Limited
Printed in Hong Kong

Contents

Introduction

The idea for a book on cake decorating has been in my thoughts for many years. I have tried to bring you my experiences of over 35 years of decorating and teaching; to pass on my ideas and methods.

For the beginners I have included step-by-step photographs and instructions. If you follow them closely they will help you over any problems you may encounter. I hope the advanced decorator will feel the freedom to experiment based upon the ideas in the book and that the blending of my ideas with yours will lead to some exciting work.

I have covered flower making in the book in three sections, starting with the simplest flowers and progressing to the more advanced flowers. Hopefully the chapter on wildfowers will bring some intersting variations to your decorating. There are also chapters on ornaments, marzipan, chocolate and of course cake making and royal icing.

As I planned the outline of the book I was reminded of the many wonderful years of pleasure cake decorating has given me and the treasured friends I have made. I hope you will also have as many hours of creative enjoyment and pleasure.

Equipment

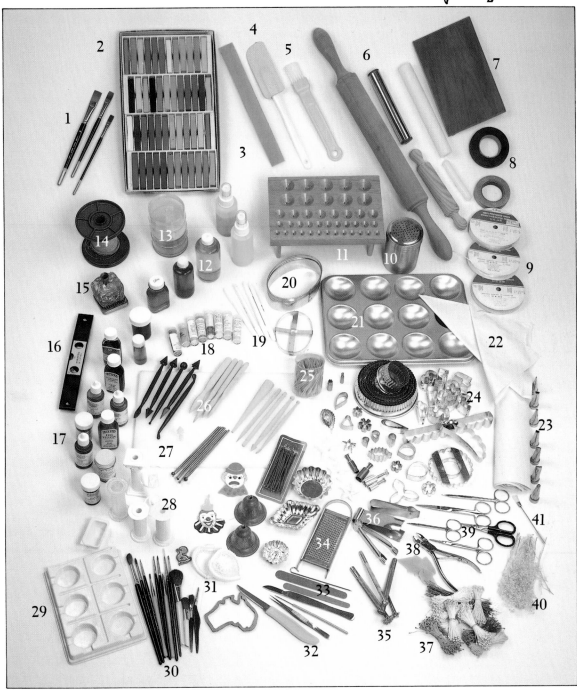

1. Nylon brushes	12. Pure alcohol and colour	23. Tubes	33. Emery boards
2. Non-toxic chalks	13. Non-toxic chalk dust	24. Cutters	34. Grater
3. Ruler	14. Wire	25. Toothpicks	35. Leather tools
4. Spatula	15. Shaping block	26. Modelling and	36. Crimpers
5. Pastry brush	16. Level	shaping tools	37. Stamens
6. Rolling pins	17. Liquid colours	27. Teflon cutting board	38. Leaf-veiners
7. Cutting board	18. Petal dust	28. Pillars	39. Scissors
8. Stemtex	19. Non-toxic pens	29. Pallets	40. Dried Baby's breath
9. Ribbon	20. Oval cutters	30. Brushes	41. Tube brush
10. Cornflour	21. Patty tins	31. Moulds	
11. Drying Stand	22. Jaconette and Jaconette bags	32. Knives and scalpels	

$\mathcal{E}$quipment and supplies for cake decorating can be obtained from either most health food stores or specialised cake decorating stores.

Icing bags

Jaconette, a material which is rubberised on one side, makes the best icing bags. Unlike nylon or plastic it does not allow the heat of your hands to penetrate it and so affect the consistency of the icing.

Care of the bag is simple; just wash it in cold water, turn it inside out and hang up to dry. As soon as the rubber starts to perish, discard the bag. Once the rubber becomes permeable the egg-white in the icing may seep through it, spoiling the consistency of the icing.

You can buy bags ready made from any health food store or make them yourself. The material is available from most large stores. A quarter of a metre of jaconette will make four 200cm bags. Cut material into four squares. Using one square, fold material diagonally, rubber-side inwards, bringing C up to B.

Machine from BC to D twice, close to the edge. Make certain the machine needle is sharp. A blunt one will make large holes and the icing could seep out through them.

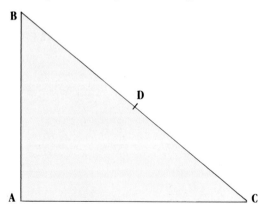

Paper icing bags

If you have to use a number of different coloured icings a disposable paper icing bag is the answer. Cut a square of greaseproof paper diagonally to make a triangle.

Roll B and C towards each other and make a tight cone with a closed point at the bottom.

Fold point A inwards and flatten paper neatly. Secure the edge with adhesive tape to maintain the shape. Cut a small hole in the point of the cone. Insert the chosen piping tube and make any necessary adjustments. Never fill the bag more than half full.

These bags can also be used without a tube by

1

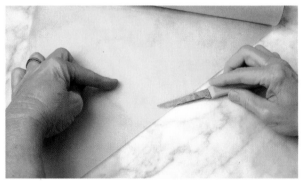

2

3

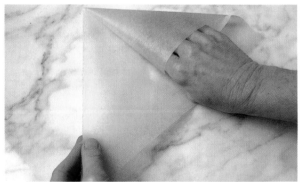

4

cutting a small hole in the point of the cone. For leaves cut away each side to form a V.

Screws or adaptors

These are inserted in the bag and allow the icing tubes to be interchanged without having to empty the bag. When a bag wears out,

remove the screw and use with a new bag. To insert the screw turn the bag inside out and push up the point as far as possible. Put the screw on the end of your finger and push right up into the point of the bag. Keep the point of the bag in the centre of the round part of the screw. If it is off centre you will have problems when the icing tube is screwed on. Take a long

5

9

6

10

7

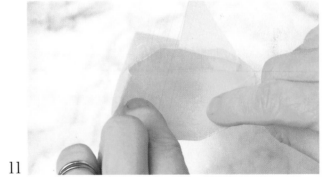

11

8

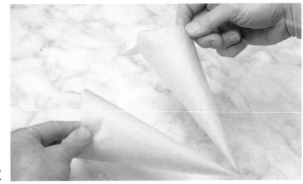

12

double thread of strong cotton and leaving a tail for tying, wind the cotton securely around the funnel part of the screw. Tie off the

cotton neatly. Turn the bag right side out and make sure the end of the screw is protruding from the point of the bag. Turn the bag back inside out, and cut and trim the bag around the edge of the screw base.

Tubes and pipes

There are many different tubes and pipes used for piping icing. They all screw on to the adaptor.

- writing tubes have plain round holes and vary in size from 00 to 4
- stars are serrated and claw-like, sizes 5 to 15
- petal or rose, left-handed or right-handed are size 20, small, medium and large
- basket weave, sizes 22 and 23
- leaf, size 16 or 17
- half-shell is size 35, small, medium and large
  A basic kit would consist of sizes 00 0 1 2 5 8 12 16 22 and 35

Icing sugar

Always use pure icing sugar. **Never** use icing mixture. It contains cornflour, which will prevent the royal icing from coming to the right consistency.

Mixing bowls

All bowls used for mixing icing should be made of glass or ceramic. Metal will discolour the icing. Plastic is too soft and gives when mixing the icing affecting its consistency.

Cake-baking tins

Tins of *various* shapes are available in aluminium and heavy galvanised tin. However you can be adventurous and invest in more unusually shaped ones — heart-shape, diamond-shape. Shop around.

Patty tins

These are used to hold the moulded flowers while they are drying so it is worthwhile buying a clean, new set. The shallow tins found in supermarkets are good enough.

Rolling pins

You can use plastic, non-stick or wooden pins for modelling. The ordinary kitchen rolling pin will do for covering a cake with almond paste, but for covering with fondant you will need a pin approximately 46cm long (not counting the handles). I prefer a turned wooden one.

Waxed paper

The cheap roll from the supermarket will do.

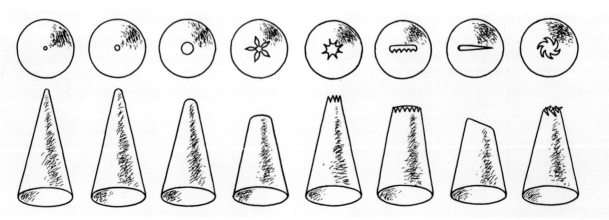

Greaseproof paper

A cheap one will do, providing it is strong as it will be used mainly for lining cake tins and making paper icing bags.

Brown paper

For lining cake tins buy a roll of brown paper sold for covering school books. It is cheap enough and there are no worries about creases.

Cake-board paper

Use good quality silver and gold paper especially made for covering boards, otherwise it can tear and mark. Never use aluminium foil to cover a cake board. It creases and tears lowering the standard of the decoration.

Adhesive paper

Stemtex and Parafilm. I use this very sparingly and prefer Stemtex.

Work board

Glazed tiles, a heavy sheet of glass or a wooden board all make a good non-stick work board for modelling and cutting out modelling paste.

Cake board

Strong masonite, not less than 3mm. If it is any lighter, the weight of the cake could cause it to bend with consequent damage to the cake decoration.

Cornflour

Use Wade's cornflour to dust your hands when modelling paste. Any other brand is too gritty. Potato flour is very good too.

Scissors

The most important are the small ones used when making flowers. They must leave your fingers easily when you wish to put them down and have a long narrow cutting edge. You will need a pair of kitchen scissors for cutting paper. Wire scissors or pliers are a must.

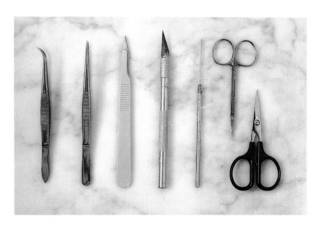

Scalpel, probe and long-nose tweezers

These are essential and can be bought from cake-decorating suppliers.

Flower cutters

The latest way to make flowers for cake decoration is to use flower cutters. There are many different ones on the market, but please learn to make the flowers freehand before you start on the cutters. This way, this wonderful creative art will survive.

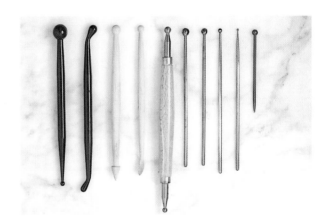

Flower shapers

The hollowing out of the paste cone to make a flower shape demands a variety of different shaped and sized tools. I use round toothpicks, hair-roller pins, golf tees and bought wooden or plastic shapes. The ball-tool is used for cupping petals. The dog-bone tool is for fluting the edges of the petals.

Moulds

There are many different sizes and shapes of mould on the market for moulding cake ornaments.

Formers

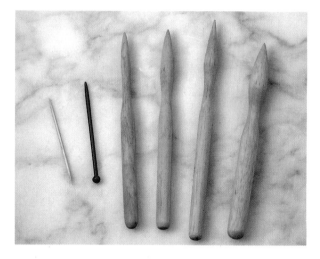

A former is coned-shaped and used to form the throat of a flower during moulding. Available in various sizes a former is made of plastic or wood.

Icing floats

These are pieces of flat board not less than 27.5cm square with a cutting edge. They are used for smoothing the almond paste or fondant covering a cake. I use a bought one or two pieces of unblemished board. A plain plastic tumbler makes a good substitute for smoothing a round cake.

Spirit-level

A miniature spirit-level will take the guesswork out of applying almond paste or fondant evenly.

Drying racks

A wooden drying rack allows the wire stem of a completed flower to pass through it and the flower to nestle in the concavity. You can buy perspex ones for drying small flowers. At a pinch you can use polystyrene foam.

Stamens

There are three kinds on the market, round-heads, half-heads and very fine heads — all have their uses, and you can choose the ones you prefer to fill the centre of your flowers. Once you have used the head of a stamen, the thread can be used by itself. Heads coloured with a darker colour look very natural.

Icing colourings

Always use the best-quality colourings available. Poor-quality colours do not contain a stabiliser and will separate and spot the fondant. Always shake the bottle well before use and use sparingly. I like the bottles of liquid colour which have an eye-dropper; they are made in England but are available here.

Pure alcohol

Pure alcohol is used to mix the colour applied to flowers made in white modelling paste or icing. Pure alcohol can be hard to obtain so I suggest you replace it with methylated spirits. It evaporates quickly leaving only the colour and, used in such minute amounts, it is virtually harmless.

Colouring chalks

These must be the special non-toxic alpha pastels. They are either grated or rubbed on to cartridge paper to form a dust, which is then applied to a modelled or piped flower with a nylon brush.

Petal dusts

These were created in England to use instead of the dust from the grated non-toxic chalks and they meet the very strict requirements of the English health laws, so they are safe to use.

Paint brushes

It is well worth spending a little extra to have a selection of top-quality brushes in different sizes. They make the work much easier.

Wire

The wire I have used for many years for wiring flowers is the rayon-covered one made locally. You can buy fine, medium or heavy wire. An English paper-covered wire is good for heavier headed flowers.

Ribbon

Ribbon is readily available, in a range of widths from very narrow to wide, and it is useful to keep different widths and colours on hand.

Lining the cake tin

$\mathcal{B}$efore you start to make the cake, line the tin. Keep the linings simple and easy to handle. I have found the following methods best.

To line a square tin:

Cut four sheets of brown paper and four sheets of greaseproof paper with a width the same size as the inside measurement of the tin from one side to the opposite one, and the length equal to the width of the base plus the depth of two sides plus 5cm.

Take two sheets of brown paper, one on top of the other, and starting about 2.5cm above the rim of the tin, take paper down one side of the tin, across the bottom and up the other side, creasing it at the bends. You should

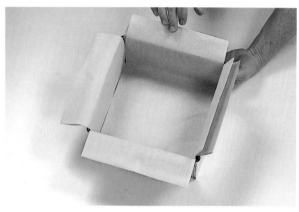

height of the tin plus 2.5cm and as long as the circumference of the tin. Do the same with greaseproof paper.

Sticky-tape the four sheets together so they can be picked up as one unit. This lining is to go round the inside of the tin.

Position it so that the bottom edge just touches the base of the tin and press it against the sides of the tin, right around the shape, creasing it into any corners if necessary.

Make sure it will hold in position by sticky-taping it from the top of the paper to the outside of the tin, as you go.

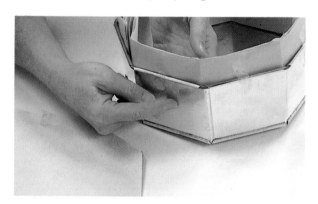

have 2.5cm protruding above the rim opposite where you started. Turn the tin 90⁰ (a half-turn) and repeat the process using the other two sheets of brown paper. The tin should now be completely covered. Do exactly the same with the greaseproof paper.

This method allows the linings to be peeled away from the cooked cake without damaging it. It is most important that the cake should be as perfectly shaped as possible.

To line a round, heart-shaped, six-sided, eight-sided or oval tin, etc

Cut a double thickness of brown paper the

Now cut two sheets of brown and two sheets of greaseproof paper to the shape of the base of the tin, and carefully insert it.

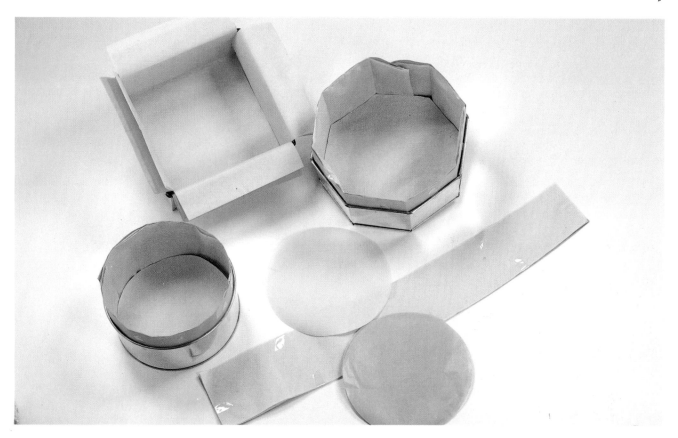

The tin is now fully lined.

The sticky-tape will probably leave marks around the tin but this method makes a perfectly shaped lining.

At one time, if you wanted a cake to be a particular shape you had to cook it in a conventional sized tin and then cut it into the shape required, and this wasted a lot of cake. Now you can get tins in all sorts of imaginative shapes and different sizes.

Tins made of galvanised heavy-duty tin cook the cakes in them more quickly than do aluminium ones. I counteract this by tying newspaper (three sheets thick) around the outside circumference of the tin. This means that the tin can be buttered and floured, or sprayed, instead of being lined. This method is very useful if you are dealing with tricky shapes.

Fruit cake

Fruit cake has plenty of body and will tolerate the handling necessary while it is being covered with almond paste and fondant. Try my recipe, it is basic but has proved to be very popular.

Let's talk briefly about ingredients. I prefer butter to margarine; castor sugar to brown sugar, and overproof rum or brandy to sweet sherry. I always use large eggs to make sure their combined weight equals that of the butter. I use plain flour, and seldom use self-raising flour. Parisian essence, in moderation, is better for giving colour than bicarbonate of soda which only just darkens the mixture. Good bought mixed dried-fruit is as suitable as the one you would mix yourself.

The quality of the fruit is very important. Raisins should be plump and big enough to be cut into four pieces. Sultanas should be at least a five crown grade; they keep the cake moist. Currants should never be less than four crown; if they are smaller, they will cook in the first hour in the oven and become dry, giving the cake a burnt taste. Always use real glacé cherries, not the imitation ones made from turnip, they cook into hard lumps. It is essential to use diced, not sliced, mixed peel.

These days all good-quality dried fruit is washed before it leaves the drying sheds, but if you insist on washing the mixture again, make sure it is thoroughly dry before you use it. Wet fruit sinks to the bottom of the cake. Our

grandmothers always soaked the fruit in rum or brandy for weeks before they made the cake. It certainly does wonders for the flavour but there could be a soaked piece of fruit near the top of the cake which you could be unlucky enough to pierce while you are covering the cake with fondant, and you would get a nasty brown mark on the fondant. I never take the risk.

Recipe (for a 21cm square cake tin or a 23cm round cake tin)

> 250g butter
> 250g castor sugar
> 1 tablespoon vanilla essence
> 5 large eggs
> 3 tablespoons overproof rum
> 360g plain flour, sifted
> 1 tablespoon Parisian essence
> 1¼kg mixed fruit
> 1 tablespoon golden syrup

This recipe can be doubled for a 26cm square tin or halved for a 15cm square tin.

Method

Cream the butter and sugar until light and fluffy then place in a large mixing bowl and add the vanilla essence. Beat the eggs, one at a time, with an electric mixer and add one at a time, to the creamed mixture, beating well after each addition. Add rum and stir it through the mixture. Gradually add the sifted flour, blending it in until evenly distributed. Add Parisian essence and stir in. Lastly add the mixed fruit and golden syrup and mix well. The mixture is now ready to be spooned into the tin.

Turn the oven on to 150⁰C or 300⁰F. While the oven is heating, spoon the cake mixture into the tin. Don't just scoop it into the middle; pack it into the sides and corners, adding the mixture until the bowl is empty.

Level the top of the mixture with a wooden spoon. Pick up the tin and drop it gently on the table. This will eliminate air bubles and allow the cake to keep level as it cooks. It is important to keep it as level as possible, for you will later turn it upside down when you cover it with fondant.

Reduce oven heat to 140°C or 275°F. Place the cake in the oven so that the top of the tin, not the paper protruding from the top of the tin, is approximately in the middle of the oven. Only do this when the required temperature has been reached. Do not open the oven door for the next two and a half hours.

To test if the cake is done, insert a pointed steak knife into the middle. Do not use a straw or a metal skewer. They are too thin to give a correct reading. The wide surface of a knife is more accurate. If the knife comes out clean, the cake is done, if it does not, put the cake back in the oven and cook a little longer. Listen to your cake to see if it is done. Cakes 'sing' while they are cooking, the singing stops when they are done.

When you are satisfied it is done, wrap it without delay, still in the tin, in a clean towel and leave it until it has completely cooled. This will take about 12 hours. On no account attempt to take the cake out of the tin until you are sure there is no heat at all left in it.

Light fruit cake

Recipe

> 250g butter
> 250g castor sugar
> 4 eggs
> 250g plain flour
> 60g self-raising flour
> ½ teaspoon salt
> 1 teaspoon mixed spice
> 1¼ kg mixed fruit
> 60g chopped almonds
> 3 tablespoons rum, sherry or brandy

Method

Cream butter and sugar together. Add the eggs, one at a time, beating well after each addition. Sift together the flours, salt and spice. Stir in the dry ingredients alternatively with the mixed fruit and almonds. Lastly add the rum and mix well. Spoon the mixture into a lined 21cm tin, bake in a slow oven for about 3½ hours. (Refer to the instructions for your own oven to determine what temperature is recommended for a 'slow oven'. This can vary according to make and type of oven.)

Problems

*I*f your cake is less than perfect you will probably have made a mistake with timing or temperature.
1. If the cake is dry and crusty on top, the oven was too hot.
2. If the top is split, the oven has been too hot. Fortunately you can remedy this. As soon as you take the cake from the oven,

place an upturned saucer over the cake and wrap the cake in the tin, in a clean towel and leave until it is completely cool. When you unwrap it you should find that the crack has closed up.

3. If the cake is too dry, it has been cooked too long.

4. If it has a wet spot in the middle of the bottom, it hasn't been cooked long enough. Fruit cakes cook slowly from the edges and the middle is the last to cook.

Sponge cake

Recipe

> 3 *eggs*
> 135g *castor sugar*
> 120g *self-raising flour*
> 1 *tablespoon butter, melted*
> 3 *tablespoons hot water*

Method

Grease two 17.5cm sandwich tins and flour lightly. Set oven temperature to 170⁰C or 350⁰F. Separate the eggs, beating the whites stiffly. Add sugar gradually, beating until mixture is thick, then add the beaten yolks. Sift the flour and fold into mixture lightly and evenly. Add melted butter and the hot water quickly and stir in. Mix thoroughly. Pour equal amounts into each of the two tins and bake in the moderate oven for approximately 20 minutes. Turn out in to a wire rack to cool. Spread chosen filling on one cake and place the other one on top.

Basic butter cake — Madeira

*T*his is the recipe to use when making cream-covered novelty cakes for the children. Bake it in a 27.5cm x 17.5cm lamington tin. You will have plenty of room to cut out all the shapes from a cake slab of this size. A packet-cake mix gives good results too.

Recipe

120g butter
135g castor sugar
1 teaspoon vanilla essence
2 eggs
250g self-raising flour
120ml milk

Method

Grease sides and line the bottom of the lamington tin. Set oven temperature at 150⁰C or 350⁰F. Cream butter and sugar until white and fluffy, add vanilla essence. Gradually beat in the lightly beaten eggs. Sift flour a couple of times and then fold into the creamed mixture alternately with the milk, starting and finishing with the flour. When the mixture is

smooth pour into the prepared tin and bake for 20 to 25 minutes. When cooked, cool on a wire rack before cutting.

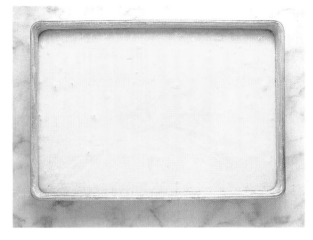

Covering the Cake

Almond paste

*I*n my opinion, the almond paste is as important as the final fondant covering, for it enables you to mend any imperfections in the shape of the cake.

Until the Second World War almond meal was always used to make the paste, but when almonds became scarce, marzipan meal was used instead. Almond meal is ground-up blanched almonds, marzipan meal is the ground-up inner kernels of stone fruit such as peaches and nectarines. Apricot kernels are

no longer used because they were found to contain cyanide. I like marzipan meal; it smells, tastes and works just like the almond meal with the added advantage that since it is less oily, it does not bleed through the fondant and leave nasty blotches as almond meal has been known to do.

Before you start to make the paste, assemble your equipment. You will need a pastry board, a pastry brush, rolling pin, a spirit level and two flat, light boards or an icing float for levelling and flattening.

Recipe

120g almond or marzipan meal
500g pure icing sugar
1 egg yolk
1 medium lemon, juiced
Same amount of sweet sherry as lemon juice
1 teaspoon glycerine
white of egg for glazing (see ' Covering the cake')

Method

Mix meal and icing sugar together in bowl. In another bowl beat the egg-yolk into the lemon juice and sweet sherry. Add the glycerine and stir in well. Add the liquid to the dry ingredients slowly, mixing as you go and continue until the dough will leave the sides of the bowl cleanly.

Sprinkle a little icing sugar on the pastry board or workbench. Put the dough on the board and roll out. If it sticks to the board, add a little more meal and icing sugar. If it is crumbly, add a little more liquid. When it rolls out nicely you are ready to begin covering the cake.

Note

The cake must be as perfectly shaped as possible. Take it out of the tin, upturn it and see if it will sit flat on the board. Since cakes do not always rise completely evenly, it probably will not. Turn the cake on its side and with a really sharp knife, cut down a little way; turn the cake slightly and make another cut level with the first one. Continue doing this until you have cut right through. The cake should now be level enough to sit flat on the board. Do not, on any account, think that

you can start at one side and cut straight through and get it even; the chances are high that you could start with a 0.5cm cut on one side and end up with a 2.5cm one on the other.

Covering the cake

1. From the rolled out paste cut a strip as wide as the height of the cake and as long as from the middle of one side and round the corner to the middle of the next one. You never put on paste from corner to corner, it must always go around the corners.

2. Glaze one side of the paste with egg-white.

3. Starting at the middle of one side, place

the glazed side of the strip against the cake and neaten into place with either the two flat boards or the icing float.

4. Repeat steps 1 to 3 for each side of the cake. Make certain the joins are as undetectable as possible.

5. Now you have to cover the top. To get the exact shape, place the cake tin on the paste, rim down, and trace round it with a sharp knife, making the cut as neat as possible. Glaze the top of the cake with egg-white, lift the cut paste carefully and place on the cake so that it fits against

the sides and makes a lid. Gently pinch the edges of the top and sides together and smooth so that no join is apparent.

6. To make the paste covering smooth, take the rolling pin gently up one side of the cake, over the top and down the opposite side. Repeat for the other side or sides.
7. When all is to your satisfaction, glaze the paste with egg-white to seal it.
8. Put a piece of waxed paper on a spare board, place the cake on it, cover, and leave to dry for at least 24 hours.
9. If you are unfortunate enough to find the

paste is uneven when it is dry, use some extra paste, glazed on one side with egg-white, to level it up.

Note

When you are attaching the paste to the cake, use just enough egg-white to make the paste sticky. If you use too much, the paste will 'float' and cause the final covering of fondant to move and separate.

Fondants

$\mathcal{F}$ondant is the final coating of the cake and therefore must be free of all marks, air bubbles or cracks. The process is called 'covering'.

Below are three recipes. The first, for super-fondant, is the one I always use. The second is a quicker one, very handy if you are icing only one cake. The third has a creamy look and is therefore better for coloured fondants than a white one.

There are a few things to bear in mind when covering.
1. Do not do it in the heat of the day.
2. Do not do it when you are tired because it can be heavy-going and if you are weary the result is likely to be poor.
3. If you wish to colour fondant, always do it in daylight, never under artificial light.
4. Make absolutely certain that your hands and work-bench are spotlessly clean.
5. Warn the family. Once you have started covering nothing must be allowed to interrupt you.
6. Don't wear a dark, fluffy jumper or anything made of material that will 'fleck' otherwise you could find some unwanted bits in the fondant.

Recipe 1 — Super-fondant

The ingredients fall into three groups:

Group 1
> 500g ordinary white sugar
> 120g liquid glucose
> 30g glycerine
> 1 level teaspoon cream of tartar
> 150ml water

Group 2
> 30g gelatine
> 150ml water

Group 3
> 120g cut-up copha butter
> 1.5kg pure icing sugar

Method

Grease the inside rim of a two litre saucepan to a depth of 2.5cm. Put the first five ingredients (group 1) into the saucepan and stir continuously over a medium heat until all the mixture has dissolved and the liquid is starting to boil. Reduce heat but keep up the boil (110°C or 240°F) until the mixture reaches a 'soft ball' consistency. Turn the heat off.

Put gelatine and water (group 2) into a second saucepan and stir over a medium heat until the gelatine has dissolved. On no account allow the liquid to boil or you will create an imbalance in the mixture, but make sure gelatine is dissolved. Turn off heat.

Add dissolved gelatine to the contents of the first saucepan, taking care that there is no overflow. Add the cut-up copha and let the mixture stand until it has dissolved. Put the mixture in a mixing bowl. You can now do one of two things...

Either add the icing sugar gradually, stirring well between each addition. Cover the bowl when everything is well mixed and leave to stand for 24 hours.

Or put the icing sugar into a heavy duty mixing bowl, add the hot mixture and using an electric mixer, mix on speed 2 for two minutes. Do not allow the mixer to labour. When all is smooth cover the bowl and leave to stand for 24 hours. There is a further process before the fondant will be ready to apply to the cake but we come to that later.

Recipe 2

1kg pure icing sugar
15g gelatine
¼ metric cup of water
½ metric cup liquid glucose
21ml glycerine
30g copha butter

Method

Sieve pure icing sugar into a bowl.
Thoroughly dissolve gelatine in the water in a
saucepan over medium heat, but do not allow
it to boil. Add glucose and glycerine to hot
liquid and stir until combined. Add copha,
allow to dissolve. Stir liquid into sieved icing
sugar. Knead in bowl until combined, then
remove from bowl and knead until smooth
and pliable. Colour if desired. It is now ready
to roll out and apply to your cake.

Recipe 3

500g pure icing sugar
1 egg-white, unbeaten
60g liquid glucose

Method

Sift the pure icing sugar into a bowl and make
a well in the centre. Add the egg-white and
warmed glucose and blend through until the
mixture can be handled. Take out of the bowl
and knead into a pliable paste which can be
rolled out and put on the cake.

If you use super-fondant, there is, as said
previously, an extra chore. You have to knead
more icing sugar into it just before you begin
to cover the cake. Take a small piece and
knead sugar into it until it becomes soft, then
do the same with another piece, and so on,
until all is used up. Now knead the whole lot
together until the fondant is white, firm, and
not in the least bit sticky. If it can hold its own
weight when it is held up and squeezed in the
middle, it is the right consistency.

Covering a cake with super-fondant

To give you an idea of the amount of
fondant you will need for the cake you
wish to cover, a 21cm square cake will take
one-third of the batch made up according to
the recipe on page 23.

Make the required amount of fondant.
Keep covered. Glaze the cake with egg-white,
making the almond paste sticky but not
sloppy. Put the cake to one side. Have your
covered cake board ready (for method see
page 23), with a small piece of waxed paper
in the middle of it.

Sprinkle sifted pure icing sugar on the
work-bench. Place the ball of fondant on the
icing sugar, sprinkle icing sugar on the ball
and knead it in. Continue the sprinkling and
kneading until the fondant has become firm,
white and not in the least sticky. By the time
it has reached the correct consistency the
original ball will have nearly doubled in size. If
you intend to have coloured fondant add the
colouring about two-thirds of the way through
the kneading process.

When you are satisfied with the
consistency of the fondant, put the ball in a
bowl, cover it, and leave it for an hour. While
you are waiting, clear up the work-bench, and
bring the cake to stand near to where you
have been working and will be working again,

covering the cake. Place your icing floats or two flat boards within easy reach.

1. Dust work-bench with icing sugar. Dust hands lightly with icing sugar.
2. Dust a 46cm rolling pin with icing sugar.
3. Roll ball of fondant on icing sugar on the bench and re-knead it gently.

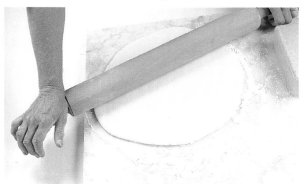

4. Roll the fondant out. To prevent it sticking to the board in the middle, and to get an even thickness, roll, then turn it a few degrees, roll and turn again. Continue doing this until you have an evenly flat sheet of fondant. Do not make the sheet too thin or any unevenness of the almond paste will show through.
5. Prick any air bubbles, and gently roll again.

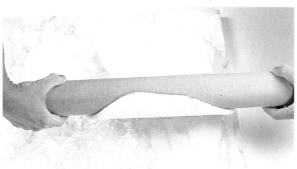

6. Pick up the sheet of fondant, just as you would a sheet of pastry, and drape it over the cake so that it is completely covered. Start at the back and bring the fondant over the top of the cake and down the other side. Consult the photographs if you are in any doubt. Some people prefer to drape the fondant over a rolling pin and lift it into place.

7. Take a flat board dusted with icing sugar and gently press the fondant down on the top of the cake. Do it carefully, as you must get rid of any air bubbles which might be under the fondant. With the cupped palms of your hands, ease the corners so that the fondant fits the cake

and gently rub them. Make sure your hands are not sticky. Use more icing sugar on them if necessary.

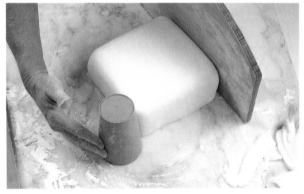

8. Using the icing floats or flat boards, cut off any excess fondant round the bottom of the cake. Do it at once, if you delay the weight of the excess fondant will pull down the fondant covering the shoulder of the cake with consequent cracking.

9. Neaten the bottom edge really well.
10. Straighten, smooth and polish the covering, using the boards, until you feel it is perfect.
11. Place the covered cake on the cake board. It is now ready to be decorated.

The process for covering the cake is just the same if you use the fondants from recipes 2 and 3.

Note
When handling the fondant make sure your hands are cool and not in the least bit sticky. Keep them lightly dusted with icing sugar.

Cake boards

A badly covered board will detract from the appearance of a decorated cake so time devoted to the job is never wasted.

Single-tier or bottom-tier boards must have cleats on the underside both to strengthen the board and to allow your fingers to fit under the edge during lifting. You can use either two strips of beading or a smaller board of the same shape. The cleats on boards used for show cakes must either be covered in the same paper as the board or painted to match.

The covering paper can be glued to the board with thick white paste, thin white paste, thin white glue or wallpaper glue. Make sure the glue is evenly distributed so that no lumps

show through and that it will not loosen around the edges. Silver and gold paper look very nice. Aluminium foil is not a suitable cover. It creases and is not strong enough.

To cover a square, six-sided, eight-sided or corner-cut board

Cut a piece of covering paper 5cm bigger all around than the size of the board and place it, wrong side up, on the table. Paste all over the smooth side of the board and place it on the paper, leaving a border of 5cm all around it. Turn board and paper over and smooth the paper down with a soft rag.

Turn the board over again. Now you have to turn the borders over so that they can be pasted to the underside of the board with the corners neatly mitred and without bumps along the edges. Take it slowly.

Carefully paste the paper protruding along one side of the board, and then turn it over and press it down evenly to the underside of the board. Do exactly the same with the opposite side. Mitre each of the four edges

in turn. Crease the paper well and keep everything as flat as possible. Paste the remaining two borders and turn them onto the underside of the board and press down, making sure all the layers of paper are firmly stuck.

Mitring is not difficult; most of us will remember being taught how to do it when we covered our school books.

To cover a round, oval, heart-shaped, blossom-shaped or any board with rounded edges

Cut the covering paper into the same shape as the board but with a 6cm margin all around. Place the paper, wrong side up, on the workbench. Paste the smooth side of the board and lower it on to the paper, centring it and leaving the margins protruding equally all around the board. Up-end the board and smooth the paper down on to it with a soft rag, making sure there are no lumps. Paste the border paper, and gathering it in to fit as you go, attach it to the underside of the board. Make certain the fit is neat and flat.

Royal Icing

Preparing the icing

*R*oyal icing is used for all piping work. You must keep shine and elasticity in the batch you are making, so follow the instructions carefully; otherwise the icing will be heavy and dull and the thread of icing will not flow easily through the piping tube.

Recipe

*1 unbeaten egg-white
pure icing sugar, sifted*

Method

1. Place the egg-white, which must be free of any yolk 'threads', and at room temperature, into a clean glass or crockery bowl.
2. Add sifted pure icing sugar, a dessertspoonful at a time, and beat with a wooden spoon between additions. Continue doing this until the mixture forms neat peaks.
3. Cover the bowl at once otherwise a crust will form on the icing. If you do get a crust, do not attempt to beat it into the batch, throw the crust away. No matter how hard you might beat, it will not blend with the rest of the icing. Remove any icing residue around the bowl so that the crusts cannot fall into the mixture.
4. If you have to leave the icing to stand for any length of time before you are ready to fill your icing bag and start work, beat the icing before you put it into the bag. The white of egg quickly settles to the bottom, so make certain it is blended in and the icing has the correct overall consistency.

If you want to colour royal icing use liquid colouring. Compensate for the liquid in the colouring by adding a little more icing sugar.

Royal icing consistency

1. *Small peak*: for general piping of dots, lines, writing, lattice, scallops, the royal icing should hold its shape when pulled to a small peak between finger and thumb.
2. *Petal consistency*: for star work with the serrated tubes and making flowers with petals that must stand up the royal icing must be stiffer. Add a couple more spoonfuls of icing sugar to small peak consistency icing. It should hold the peak up on the back of the spoon as it is lifted from the bowl.
3. *Soft peak*: is a little looser than the small peak mixture and is used for embroidery, lace and extension work.

Problems

1. If the mixture is too soft add more pure icing sugar.
2. If it is too heavy add just a touch of egg white to bring it back to the right consistency.
3. If it is dull and heavy you have added too much icing sugar too quickly and have not beaten it well enough between additions.
4. Never use icing mixture. This has cornflour in it and will give you an incorrect consistency.
5. I do not believe you should keep the royal icing in the refrigerator because the covered bowl can form condensation and the recipe does not call for water.

Learning how to use the icing bag and tubes

*Y*ou have to learn how to hold the bag, how to apply pressure so that the icing will emerge from the tube nozzle steadily and not in fits and starts, how to make straight lines, both upwards and downwards, to make loops and dots and lattices, to write names and numbers, and you have to familiarise yourself with different types of tube and the consistency of the icing needed for them. Only practice will enable you to do all this, so do not feel it is a waste of icing and time if all you do for a while is to make practice patterns on a plain masonite board. It is important to gain perfect control; some people manage it more quickly than others, but as long as you get there, why worry? Patience always pays off.

To fill a bag with royal icing, fit the chosen tube on to the bag, turn the top half of the bag over the outside. Lay the bag across your left hand and spoon in the royal icing.

Turn the top half of the bag back up and squeeze the icing down the bag. Twist the top half of the bag around.

It is best to begin with a writing tube. Attach it to the adaptor in the bag. The sizes run from 00, 0, 1, 2 and 3. Start with the largest one. Fill the bag with icing and fold the top over as instructed. Place the bag across your hand with the folded top just under the thumb muscle, close your four fingers around the bag and keep your thumb on the folded top.

The pressure to force the icing through the tube must come from your fingers, not from the thumb. Squeeze the bag and a thread of icing will emerge, stop the pressure and the thread will not come out. Hold the bag with your elbow lifted and the nozzle of the tube pointing downwards, squeeze the bag gently and, as the thread begins to emerge, guide it in the direction you wish it to go. Using a large writing tube, practise making straight lines first; then add some loops and dots.

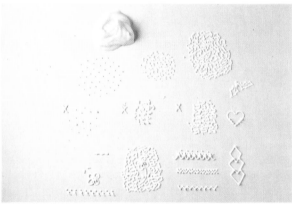

When you begin to feel confident, you can move on to the star and petal pipes and the fine writing tubes. For writing and embroidery hold the bag at a 45^0 angle, and for stars and dots hold it at a 90^0 angle.

If you find the icing is beginning to blob and the stars are indistinctly marked, the icing has become too soft. You will have to take it out of the bag and beat it again, possibly adding a little more icing sugar.

Edging

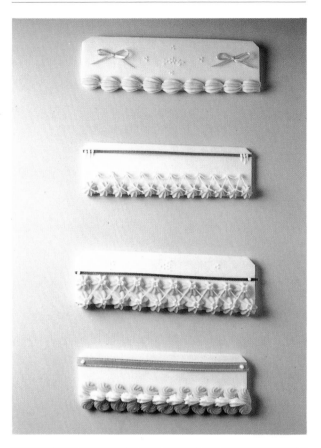

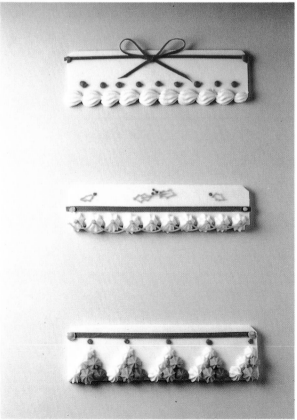

*E*dgings, or borders as some people call them, are very important to the look of the finished cake. When you come to make them you will see how essential it was to neaten the bottom edges of the cake and to make sure that the coverings of almond paste and icing were smooth, level and as exact as you could make them.

Borders round the bottom edges of a cake are piped with royal icing. The simplest edging is the shell pattern. The icing must be stiff enough (petal consistency) for the shell shape to be clearly defined — if the icing is too soft the edges of the design will 'blur'. The shells must be of equal shape and size, and should overlap, each shell taking in the tail of the preceding one. You can be as imaginative as you like in designing the borders and making patterns using the different tubes. The plain writing tube comes in very handy here.

Lace

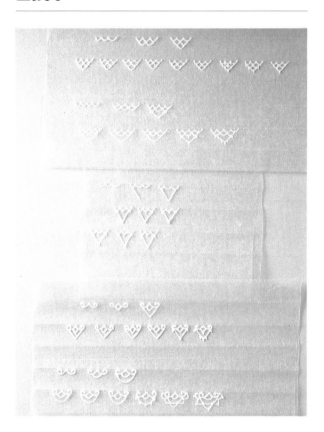

*T*his is made on creased wax paper. Fold the sheet of paper in half and then crease it in parallel lines approximately 1.25cm apart. Do not concertina the paper, it must lie flat

on the workbench. Use creased waxed paper because this allows the icing to dry easily and to be picked up easily when the lace pattern is made. Fill the icing bag with royal icing of a soft peak piping consistency and screw a 00 writing tube to the adaptor. Lace is made using loops, dots, scrolls, etc and it is important to work slowly and carefully. Make sure that each stroke joins.

Hold the bag at an angle as shown in illustration on page 30. Pipe slowly, pressing the bag all the time and feeling the paper lightly under the tube end. Lace is piped from the straight edge downwards. This allows the loops to flow in a more natural curve than if you were working in the opposite direction and taking them upwards. Make sure that each stroke joins the previous one so that the finished lace can be picked up in one piece.

You do not have to pipe a long straight edge to make a top border for the lace. A long straight edge would make the completed lace bulky and hard to handle when you attach it to the wet joining thread used to attach it to the cake. When you pipe your first row make sure that no icing protrudes above the crease in the paper which you take as your guide. Make sure that you keep the paper straight or the finished lace will be at a slant and it will not be usable.

Embroidery

Designs for finely piped embroidery for the top and sides of a cake can be copied from those found on material, lace, baby clothes, tablecloths and embroidery transfers. As you become more proficient you will even be able to use the design of a bride's dress as your pattern or to follow the floral theme of the bouquet and will find making dainty animals suitable for a christening cake no problem.

You can build up the design, stroke by stroke, if you feel confident enough, but if working freehand is too daunting, trace your chosen design on to greaseproof paper and retrace it on to the fondant of the cake, using a knitting needle. It is hardly necessary to say, go carefully.

Use a 00 writing tube and make sure the icing is at soft peak consistency, and **practice.** Some people prefer to use a paper cone instead of an icing bag and hold it as they would a pencil.

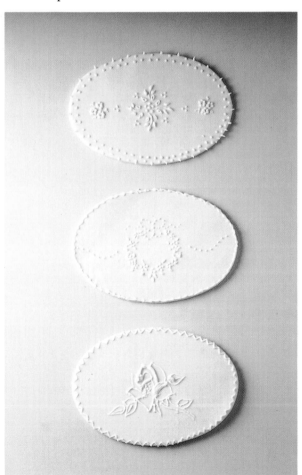

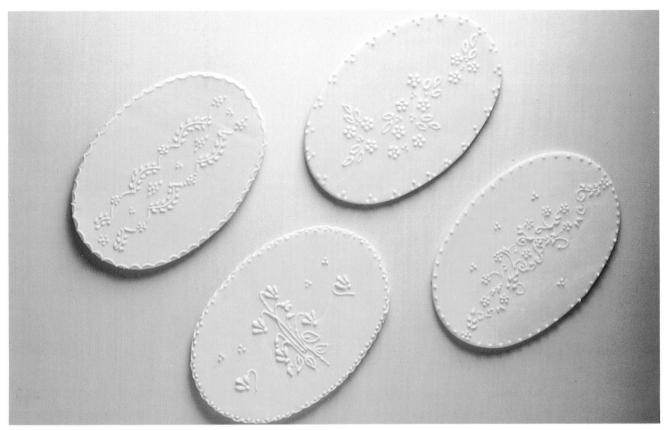

The first exercises should be making loops, lines, dots, stems, leaves, tear-drops and a simple flower like the forget-me-not. Using a light touch, feel the fondant under the tube as you work. If the designs run, and start to look messy the icing is too soft, you will have to start again after you have thickened it with a little more icing sugar.

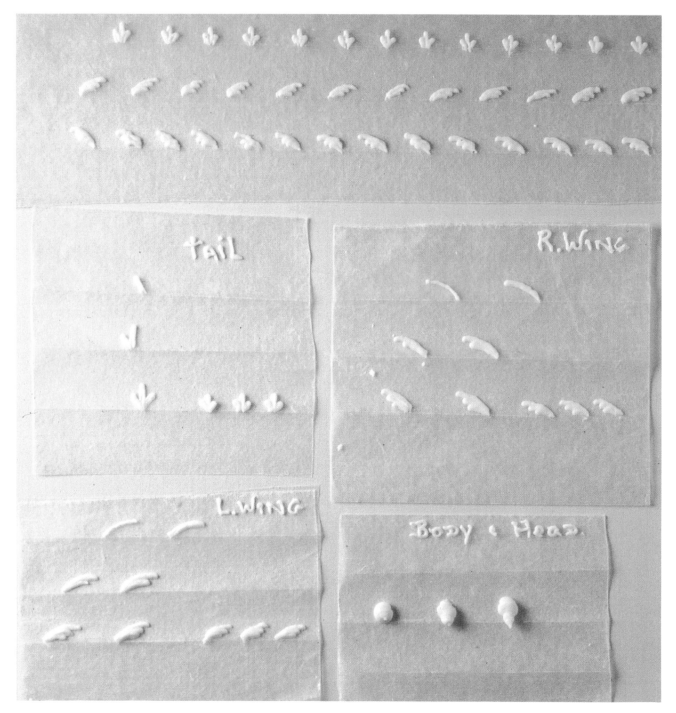

Bluebirds and doves

*T*hese are cute little birds which can perch on the top or the side of a cake. Doves are made of plain white royal icing, bluebirds from royal icing which has been coloured a pale baby-blue. When making bluebirds, make an entire bird from the same batch of icing, otherwise you could get a two-toned one. Do not forget to make a spot of colour for tiny eyes.

Making the birds

You will need a batch of royal icing, a sheet of wax paper, the icing bag fitted with a 00 tube.

Fold the wax paper in half, then crease it in parallel lines approximately 1.25cm apart. Do not concertina the paper. It must lie flat on your working surface. Add a dessertspoon of sifted pure icing sugar to the icing you have made, which should be of medium peak piping consistency. You need the extra stiffness so that you can give the tail and wings of the bird a genuinely feathered look. Put the icing in the bag.

The tail

The tail is made up of three feathers, a long one in the centre and a shorter one each side of it. Begin with the outside left feather. Starting at the centre crease of the waxed paper, pipe at a 45⁰ angle to the left, and without stopping the flow of icing come back to the starting point, then pipe the middle feather — go out straight, making the feather slightly longer than the first one. Come back to the starting point and then pipe the right-hand feather at a 45⁰ angle to match the first one. All this must be done in one continuous flow.

Right wing

Using a continuous thread of icing and working to the right, make three slightly overlapping loops of diminishing size, all finishing at the starting point.

Left wing

Do exactly the same but work in the opposite direction.

Place the wings on one side and allow to dry thoroughly.

Body

Keep the piping tube at an angle, and squeeze out a 'body' shape. Release the pressure and move the tube slightly forward, pipe a little

head and pull up quickly so that the icing forms a beak. The head should, of course, be attached to the body.

Assembling

While the body is still wet, attach the dry tail, then carefully place the dry wings, one each side of the body starting just below the head. You know the shape of a bird — follow it as closely as you can.

Note
Two birds on any one cake are sufficient.

Moulded Flowers

Modelling pastes

*M*ost of the ornaments used to decorate cakes are made from pastes which are variations of a type of gum paste the Greeks used for their confectionery many generations ago. I use two different recipes.

Recipe 1

This is excellent for fine work, but once made, you have to add more icing sugar to it before you can model it.

Ingredients

30ml water
2 level teaspoons gelatine
1 rounded teaspoon liquid glucose
150g pure icing sugar

Method

Heat the water and gelatine in a small saucepan over medium heat. Stir with a teaspoon until the gelatine is completely dissolved. Do not allow the mixture to boil·or the liquid balance of the recipe will be lost.

Turn off the heat. With the hot teaspoon take up a rounded spoonful of liquid glucose and stir it into the mixture. Pour mixture into a clean bowl. Add the pure icing sugar, a spoonful at a time, and beat in well after each addition. When the mixture is smooth, cover the bowl and leave it for eight hours.

Recipe 2

This recipe includes gum tragacanth, an ingredient not used here as often as it is in other countries. The recipe does not require the addition of more icing sugar once it is made, and for this reason, I like it, but since it has a higher fat content than the first recipe, it is harder to colour.

Ingredients

> 500g pure icing sugar
> 1 level teaspoon gum tragacanth
> 3 level teaspoons gelatine
> 50ml water
> 2 level teaspoons liquid glucose
> 2 level teaspoons copha butter

Method

Use a wooden spoon and a crockery or glass bowl. Place the icing sugar and gum tragacanth in the bowl and mix together. Dissolve the gelatine in the water in a small saucepan over medium heat. Make sure the liquid does not boil. Take saucepan away from the heat and add the liquid glucose and the copha butter to the dissolved gelatine and stir until the mixture is smooth.

Pour mixture slowly into the icing sugar mixture and mix until the resultant paste is stiff enough to handle. Take paste out of the bowl and knead on a board lightly covered with icing sugar until all the ingredients are well combined. Put the ball of paste into a plastic bag and put the plastic bag into a sealed container and leave for 48 hours. It will then be ready to use.

Problems

1. If the paste is greyish you did not heed the instructions and used a metal spoon or metal container.
2. If the paste is heavy and rubbery with no pull in it, you have added too much gelatine.

Note
Measurement of the ingredients used in these two recipes must be precise, otherwise the consistency of the paste will be wrong and you will find it very difficult to use.

General techniques

Bean and cone shapes

These are the basic shapes from which most small flowers are made.
1. Roll paste into a 3mm ball.
2. Form the ball into a cone shape by rolling the ball lengthways and shaping a point at one end and a rounded top at the other.
3. Using a toothpick hollow-out the cone ready to make a flower.

Long and short cuts

The size of the petal is determined by the length of the cuts made in the rim of the cone

of paste. A short cut for a small petal would be approximately 3cm deep. A long cut for a large petal would be 6cm deep.

Five equal cuts

Cut the first petal to size, then cut one of equal size on each side of it. Make the last cut to halve the remaining piece.

Mending petals

Whether you cut the paste with a knife, cutter or scissors the edges always look a little torn so gently smooth them between your thumb and index finger to give a natural look.

Petal thickness

When you hollow out a cone of paste to make a flower shape, the thickness of the petals will be determined by how thin you make the paste around the upper rim.

Mitring

This is the term used for cutting a petal into shape. A long mitre makes a pointed petal. A short mitre makes a snub-nosed petal. A round mitre a gently rounded petal.

Fluting (3 methods)

1. Place the moulded petal on a flat board and gently run a dog-bone tool around the petal edges.
2. Place the petal on the board as above, then place a round toothpick so that a small part of its length lies on the petal and the rest on the board. Roll it gently to and fro, pressing in the part of the toothpick on the board, not the part on the petal.
3. This is the method I use most. Take the upper edge of the petal between thumb and forefinger. Push the finger forward and at the same time pull the thumb backwards. Practise on thick paste to begin with and as you get the feel of it, use thinner and thinner paste. Once you have mastered the technique you can vary the shape of the fluting.

Wiring

A wire with a hooked end is used for wiring most flowers and all buds. The exception is a bell-shaped flower. Knot the wire leaving the length needed below the knot. Trim the knot so that no wire protrudes from it and it can be drawn down to the base of the bell without spoiling the shape. To wire a large flower such as a daffodil, make a wired calyx, dampen it and attach it to the base of the dry flower.

Drying

Pierce holes in the bottom of a block of paste so that it can dry from the inside. If left to dry from the outside, gas will form inside the block and either split it open or crack it badly.

Arranging

No 1 size flowers are the large ones which make the focal point of a spray, eg frangipanis, roses, daisies.

No 2 size flowers are smaller flowers used to accompany the main flowers. Six or more are used together to make a spray, eg japonica, mint ladies.

No 3 size flowers are called 'filler flowers'. Groups of three tiny flowers and a bud fill in the very smallest spots. Groups of three flowers about the size of a one cent piece and a bud accompany a larger flower.

Flower centres

Always use plenty of stamens. Wherever possible I prefer to remove the stamen heads and just use the threads. I paint the tips a dark colour and find this gives a very natural look.

Never let any of the royal icing used to hold the stamens in place be visible when the flower is finished.

If the flower has a domed centre — ie carnation, take particular care in the way you fit the petals together.

Buds

Buds can be:
- short and bulbous
- short and pointed
- long and thin

The shape of the flower will indicate the shape of the bud.

1. Place a small ball of damp modelling paste

and lengthen bud over the hooked end of a piece of wire and firm it into shape paying particular attention to the bottom part of the ball which must fit the wire closely. Shape the top part of the bud.

2. Paint a tiny calyx of the palest green at the bottom of the bud. Do not make the colour heavy. Too much heavy green in a delicate flower arrangement can be overpowering and looks wrong, particularly in a design for a wedding cake. Paint the folded petals at the top of the bud to match the flower colours. Some buds are all green, especially the short bulbous ones in which the petals have not yet begun to open.

Leaves

You can use special cutters to make the leaves but they are simple to mould freehand. The best way of all is to press a real leaf on to wet paste — you have shape, veining and imprint all in one go. Cut out the leaves and mark the veins to make them look as natural as possible. If the leaf has a serrated edge make the tiny cuts with the well-sharpened end of a small narrow knife. The cuts must be clean. Never leave a leaf flat. In the natural state they all have slight curves of one sort or another.

Leaf colouring is very important. If the scheme of your design is the darker colours, the natural colour of the leaves will look right, but if the flowers are pale, the dark green of the leaves could be overpowering, so use your discretion, both for the depth of colouring and the number of leaves you use.

Dainty Bess

$\mathcal{T}$he flower from which the shape is taken is the dog rose, which has five petals, as long as they are wide, and a centre filled with stamens. I take the heads off bought stamens and tip the stalks with a darker colour, the

flower looks more natural if only the stems are used.

Note
The scissors, knife or cutters used to cut out the petals will tear the edges slightly. Mend

the edges by patting them gently between thumb and forefinger, making them look soft and natural.

Making the flower

1. Take a ball of white or coloured modelling paste the size of a one cent coin and gently roll into a bean shape.
2. Keep a point at one end and a rounded smooth one at the other, pat gently to flatten. Finger the rounded edge carefully to make it look natural.

3. If the petal has become longer than it is wide, cut it into shape, starting half-way down one side and finishing half-way up the other. Do not cut the rounded edge.

Shaping the petal

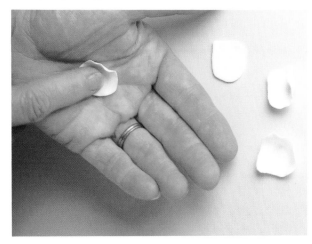

You can do this in four different ways.
1. Place the petal in the centre of the palm of your left hand. Keeping the hand loose, press the thumb or finger of your right hand on to the paste so that it 'cups'. Do not close the left hand over the petal.

2. Gently press a dog-bone tool around the outer edge of the petal.

3. Flute the edge of the petal, using a rounded toothpick, then cup the petal as for 1.

4. Finger-flute the edges of the petal and cup.

Leave completed petals to dry.

Colouring the petal

You can make the petal in coloured paste, or in white paste which you will colour, using colour mixed with pure alcohol or methylated spirits. When colouring the centre of the flower — start your brush stroke at the point in the centre of the bottom of the petal and bring it upwards, stopping half way up the petal. Without delay, using thumb or finger, stroke the colour upwards so that there is no hard line where it ends.

Assembling the flower

Always work on waxed paper. This gives support and enables the flower to be peeled away easily. Take a square of waxed paper and put a dab of royal icing in the middle of it. Don't make the dab too big. Place the point at the base of the first petal in the royal icing, then slightly overlapping the petals as you go, add the remaining four petals, with the last one tucked under the first. Remove any excess royal icing and fill the centre of the petals with stamens, one at a time. Use plenty of stamens. A double Dainty Bess has a second row of smaller petals inside the first row.

Problems

1. If you have pressed the petal so that it is long and narrow rather than square, trim it into shape.
2. If the icing has become dry and cracked you have been fingering it for too long. Discard the petal and start again.
3. If the petal is too folded you have not left your left hand loose enough when cupping it.
4. If the cupping looks stiff and unnatural, place the ball of your finger close to the top edge of the petal and cup again.
5. Can you see royal icing around the stamens? If you can, you have left too much there before inserting them. When you look down into the flower only the stamens should be in view.

Lilies

The Arum lily is white with a yellow tongue. The yellow lily is white with touches of green and darker yellow tongue. The petals of the chestnut-brown lily are pale plum colour inside and chestnut-brown outside, the tongue is pale yellow. You can use them together in a spray or singly to expand a spray of other flowers.

Arum lily

Tongue

Make a tongue from yellow modelling paste. Wire it and lightly touch the whole tongue with egg-white and then dip it into yellow powdered non-toxic chalk or petal dust and allow to dry.

Flower

1. Make a petal from a long bean of white modelling paste (about 2.5cm) and shape to a point at each end. Flatten. Wet the centre with water in a thin line from the middle of the petal to the bottom and place the dry, wired tongue along the wet area, starting about a third of the way down the petal.
2. Wrap the bottom right side of the petal over the bottom half of the tongue and secure it in place with a touch of water. Fold the left side over and neaten down on to the wire. Gently ease the top point of the petal back a little.

Yellow lily

Make in the same way as for the Arum lily but place the tongue lower down the petal and keep the fold lines to the centre front when you wrap the petals over. Gently pinch the top of the petal and pull it back gently to extend it. Tip the pinched point of the petal with green and apply a soft green water wash to the back of the flower from the base to the tip.

Chestnut-brown lily

Make the tongue longer and thinner than for the other two lilies. Fold the edges of the petals over the tongue, keeping the fold to the centre. Colour the outside of the flower with chestnut brown non-toxic chalk and the inside with light-plum coloured non-toxic chalk. Apply a wash of green up the back of the flower from the base to the tip.

If you look through your gardening books you will find lilies of other colours which are easy to model.

Open rose

*T*his flower should not be confused with a double Dainty Bess.

The open rose has five rows of petals.

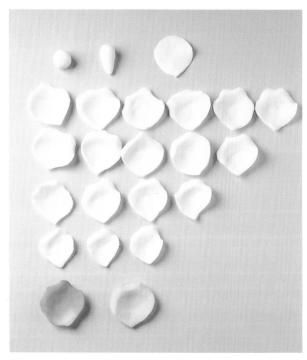

There are three small petals in the inner most row, four larger ones in the next, five larger ones still in the next, etc. The outer row has seven large petals. The centre of the flower is filled with stamens.

Take a real rose petal and study the shape. It is not deeply concave. Study the way the petals of a real rose fit together. You will need 25 petals for each rose, so estimate the amount of modelling paste you will need as accurately as you can. Model the three small petals first, and place them on one side. Then model the four larger ones and do the same. Then the five, six and seven petals needed for the other rows. Leave them all to dry.

The method used to model the petals is the same for all sizes:

1. Take the bean of white modelling paste and flatten it between thumb and forefinger, keeping the shape reasonably square.
2. Place the paste petal over the pad of your thumb so that a 3cm margin is left at the top.
3. Take the margin gently between the thumb and index finger of your other hand and turn it back, away from the thumb holding the petal. Do this in two or three different places. Do not pinch the paste. Make the curve smooth. Place the petal on the work-bench. It will have the shallow concave shape of a real rose petal.

Assembling the petals

Press an 8cm square of wax paper into a patty pan and using a No. 5 star tube, make a circle of royal icing, the size of a 20 cent coin, in the centre of it. Place the seven outside petals in the royal icing, curved edge to the outside, and arranged so that they fit with each other and are standing, rather than lying back.

Now keeping the slightly upright shape, add the other petals one row at a time. Leave enough room in the centre for the stamens.

I use the thread of the stamen and tip it with a darker colour. Work as quickly but as efficiently as you can so that the royal icing cannot dry out before you have finished.

I coloured petals of the roses in the photographs before they were assembled. The darker one had the back and front of the petals coloured yellow with non-toxic chalk, then with pink non-toxic chalk darkening the outer edge, and yellow at the centre tip.

The lighter one was coloured with a paintbrush and colours mixed with pure alcohol. The petals are yellow, the tips shading to pink.

Roses made on a plastic mould

*T*his method is ideal for beginners, it is not only easy but as you use it, you really learn how a rose is constructed. You need a plastic sweetheart rose — most chain stores have them. If you buy two, you can use one to make the moulds and keep the other as a pattern.

Method

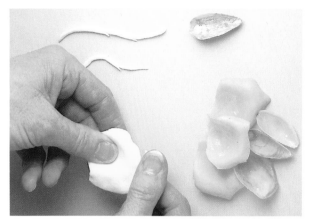

1. Pull plastic rose apart and lay the petals on the workbench, keeping the ones from each row together.
2. Inspect each one and remove any protruding bits of plastic. Dust each one, on both sides with cornflour.
3. Pat out a ball of modelling paste as thinly as possible. Take a small piece of paste and one plastic petal and lightly press the paste on to the petal and cut away any excess around the edges. You may find that the

edge of the petal will do the cutting for you.

4. Take the paste petal out of the plastic one, redust the plastic one with cornflour and replace the paste petal in it.
5. Continue in the same way with all the remaining petals. Keep them laid out on the workbench, each row of petals together, and leave to dry. Always make one extra centre petal.

Assembling the petals

Place a dab of icing at the base of each of the four centre petals. Using the icing as 'cement' fit the four petals together and hold in place for about five seconds. Turn the shape bottom-side up and fill the gaps with royal icing. This step is very important. This centre will be the basis of the remaining petals. Allow it to dry thoroughly before proceeding to the next step. Keep an eye on your sample rose and notice how the petals fit in with each other. Add each row of petals using the same method. The royal icing used to fill the gaps should be kept at the base of the petals and should not be seen when you look down into the rose.

Important
Make sure the icing used for each row is thoroughly dry before you go on to the next step. When the rose is assembled, put it in a patty tin and leave to stand for 24 hours.

Colouring

A rose usually has a basic colour — white, pink, red — but the petals can be tinged with other colours or carry deeper tones of its own. You can colour the petals in different ways.

1. You can mould the petals in modelling paste coloured pink, cream or red and use chalks to make the lighter or darker markings.
2. You can use white modelling paste to make the petals and then colour them with chalk, liquid colour or petal dust. The paste petals must have been left to dry for 24 hours before colouring of any sort is undertaken.

Note
When you can make this rose successfully, you can go on to making a standard rose. In the meantime you will find this one very useful used with a moulded bud, stalks and leaves.

Primulas

*P*rimulas are small flowers, easy to make, with clean simple colours ranging from white to pale mauve or pink. They have a tiny speck of yellow in the centre. They are only used as 'fillers' or to soften a spray of other flowers.

Method

1. Shape a 65mm bean-shaped piece of modelling paste into a cone.
2. Using a round toothpick, hollow out the cone.

5. Round the top of the petals using thumb and forefinger and flatten each one slightly. You now have five heart shaped petals.

6. Wire the flower through the centre. Bring up the centre a little and flatten back the

3. Make five short cuts into the rim of the cone to form five equal sized petals.

4. Press into each petal and with the blade of a knife dent each one down the centre.

petals to make a shallow cup. If you make the flower this way you will not have to mitre the petals.

7. Colour the centre of the flower yellow with colour straight from the bottle and leave it to dry thoroughly, otherwise it will 'bleed' into the colour of the petals. Mix the petal colour with pure alcohol and paint the back of each petal. The colour will seep through the paste and tint the upper side.

The bud is small and bulbous. These flowers and a bud make a nice spray.

Verbena

*T*he darker shades of the verbena make it a very useful 'filler' flower to include in sprays of larger darker flowers. All the flowers have a yellow-specked centre and a white eye, so I always make them in white modelling paste.

Method

1. Take a small bean-shaped piece of paste about 65mm long and mould it into a small cone.
2. Hollow out the centre with a rounded toothpick.

3. Make five short cuts of equal length into the rim of the cone to make five equally-sized petals.

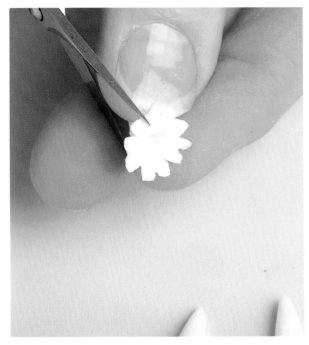

4. Holding the flower, open out the petals slightly and dent each one once with an open scissor blade or knife. Make sure the dent is in the centre of the petal.

5. Press the top corners of the petal gently with the fingers and then flatten the paste. You will now have a flower with five heart shaped petals.

6. Using a tiny ball-tool make the centre of the flower quite deep.
7. Wire, using a very small hook at the head of the wire and allow to dry.

To colour

1. Use colour either mixed with water or pure alcohol.
2. Paint the back of the petals with a lighter

shade of the main colour. Allow to dry.

3. Paint in the yellow centre of the flower. Allow to dry.

4. Paint the front of the petal with the main colour, leaving a white 'eye' around the hollowed centre and working from the centre to the edge of each petal.

You are unlikely to need just one verbena so make a number of flowers and paint them in different colours and make into a spray.

Ballerina rose

*T*his climbing rose from the musk family flowers in huge clusters and is very easy to model. The delicate colouring makes it ideal for cake decoration. Always make it in white modelling paste and colour the petals on the back with colouring mixed with pure alcohol so that the colour can seep through the paste and give the flower its typical soft pink glow.

Method

1. Make a 90mm bean-shaped piece of paste and flatten it slightly.
2. Indent the rounded edge in the centre to make a heart-shaped petal.
3. Flatten again.
4. Make four more petals in exactly the same way. Curve the heart-shape top slightly inward. Leave the petals to dry.

5. Take a small square of greaseproof paper, place point Bb on point B. Hold the pleat which is formed in place with a dab of royal icing at its point.
6. Arrange the five petals in the royal icing, each one overlapping the next at the centre.
7. Fill the centre with yellow stamen threads tipped with brown. Use just enough royal icing to keep them firm but no more.
8. Using pink colour mixed with pure alcohol, paint the back of each petal with a fine brush. Keep colour strongest at the top of each petal. Leave to dry.

Hyacinth

*A*lthough it is the most commonly used filler flower, the hyacinth is not easy to make. This method eliminates some of the mitring and shaping usually considered necessary. The flower has six petals and comes in several colours. It is one of the very few blue ones used in cake decorating. You can make it in white paste and colour it later with colour mixed with pure alcohol or make it in coloured paste.

Method

1. Hollow out a small bean of white paste with a round toothpick to make a small cone.
2. Using scissors make a long cut from the rim of the cone towards the bottom.

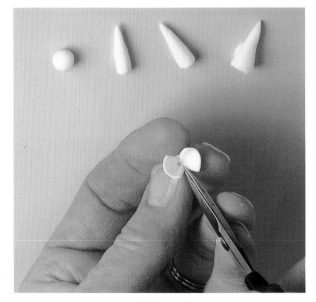

3. Make a second cut opposite the first one.

4. The cone now has two halves. Make three deep cuts into each half so that you have six petals.

6. Mark the centre of each petal lengthwise with the back of a knife or scissors.

5. Snip off the top corners of each petal.

7. Squeeze the point of each petal, flatten and gently squeeze again. Turn each petal outwards very slightly. Do not pinch the whole petal or the flower will end up looking like a spider.
8. Wire the flower and gently make the centre deeper.

Frangipani

$\mathcal{S}$ome people seem to have trouble with the shape of the petals of this lovely flower but you will find the following method very easy. Make the flower in white paste and colour it when it is dry.

Method

1. Take a bean of paste about 2.5cm long and shape it so that it tapers to a point at the bottom, and is nicely rounded at the top.

2. Flatten into shape.

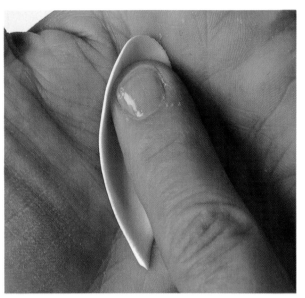

3. Shape the petal. Place it in your left hand, just below the pad of the thumb, run your finger down the length of the petal, exerting gentle pressure — just enough to make the edge of the top side turn slightly inward.

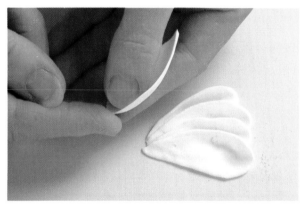

or

Place the petal along the inside of your index finger, place your thumb along it, leaving a small margin, then roll that small margin over towards the thumb. You will now have a turned edge across the top of the petal and down the left-hand side.

4. Make another four petals in exactly the same way.

5. Wet each petal on the right-hand side (the one which has not been curled) to about a quarter way up.

6. Keeping the top of the petals level, lay the second one on the first, the third on the second and the fourth on the third and fifth on the fourth, overlapping as in the above photograph.

7. Pick up the joined petals, wet the right hand side of the fifth petal to about quarter way up, wrap it round to overlap the back of the first petal by about a third.

8. Roll the bottom of the flower where the thinnest part of the petals join, between thumb and finger, squeezing gently to make sure they hold together and making a slight spiral at the centre of the flower.

9. Hold the flower upright and coax the petals into shape.

10. To support it while it dries, insert into a hollow plastic bottle-stopper. If you cut the stoppers into different heights you can vary the shape of the flowers. The lower the support the more open the flower will dry.

11. When completely dry, colour the centre with an old brush dipped in yellow chalk. It is safer to use dry colour as liquid colour can seep up the petal and leave a water-mark.

Sweet pea

*T*he flower is simple to make and since it is found in both dark and delicately pale colours it is very useful when a spray is needed. Use white paste rolled as thin as possible to keep the ethereal look of the flower. I use English paper-covered wire to assemble the flower.

Method

1. Take a pea-sized piece of modelling paste and shape it into a crescent.

2. Insert a tightly hooked piece of wire into one of the pointed ends of the crescent and leave to dry.

3. Make a Dainty Bess shaped petal and widen it slightly with a rolling pin. Finger-flute the edges.

4. Wet the wired crescent on the back and wrap the petal around it, neatening the join at the base and curving the petal so that it stands up and out a little.

5. Make a second Dainty Bess petal but larger and wider than the first one. Finger-flute the edges.
6. Wet the bottom half of the petal in the centre and wrap it round the other petal to make a larger back petal and ease it back away from the first petal encircling the crescent.

To colour

Spray the whole flower with colour mixed with pure alcohol.

Carnation

*T*he carnation is a bulky flower, so the modelling paste used must be as thin as possible. To shape the flower I used a spiked flower-holder with a 10cm by 10cm square block of plasticine pressed down on to the spikes. Into this I insert a hollow tube and into the tube I press a square of alfoil with my little finger. I then shape the alfoil protruding from the top of the tube so that it will support the petals of the flower I am about to make.

Flower

1. Take a small bean of modelling paste of about 1cm and flatten it into a tear-drop shape. Finger-flute the top edge. Do not worry if you tear it. It makes the petal look more natural. Make approximately 12 petals.

2. Wet the alfoil at the base of the tube, insert the pointed end of the petal and ease the top back over the alfoil.
3. Insert the next petal, slightly overlapping the first and continue around the tube until a slightly oval shape is formed.
4. Make a second row of petals, alternating them with the first and keeping them slightly upright.

5. Continue filling towards the centre in the same manner until the centre is slightly domed. It should not be flat.
6. The flowers can be coloured red, pink, magenta, yellow, etc, but not blue. Use colour straight from the bottle or mixed with pure alcohol.

Calyx

Hollow a 2.5cm cone of white paste and make five short cuts in the rim. Mitre each sepal and flatten slightly. If you wish to wire the flower, insert the wire now and attach calyx to the back of the flower by slightly dampening the inside of the cone. Otherwise just dampen the calyx and attach it to the base of the flower.

Leaves

The colour of the calyx and leaves is a green I have always found difficult to mix. Try leaf-green mixed with blue and add a speck of black.

Violet

*T*he easiest way to make a violet is in one piece from a cone of paste. They have a little white face in the centre, so make them in white paste and colour them afterwards. Violets are not always deep purple, they can be much paler and softer, so vary the colouring when you make a spray.

Flower

1. Hollow out a 60mm cone of white paste with the head of a hair-roller pin.
2. Cut the top of the rim, make a long cut with a shorter cut each side of it and close

enough to form two 'ears'. Gently turn back the ears.

3. Make a cut on each side of the ears to form a wider petal. This will take you to slightly more than half way down the circle.
4. Curve the bottom of the circle of paste outward to form the bottom petal of the violet.
5. Mitre the ears and flatten slightly.

6. Mitre the side petals, maintaining the width. Flatten and twist gently sideways. Not a lot, but enough to take the flatness out of the flower.

7. Using the ball end of the roller pin, curve the bottom petal slightly upwards.

Bud

Shape a long thin bud on to the end of the wire and flatten slightly. Firm into place. Curve the wire so that the bud faces downwards.

Colouring

Using paint straight from the bottle paint the back of the flowers. Leaving a white area at the base of each petal to make the white central 'eye' of the violet, paint the front of the petal from the eye outwards, making certain the edges of the petal are coloured. Leave to dry.

Using a non-toxic cake-decorating pen draw in tiny black stripes in the white area of the bottom petal. Pipe in a dot of royal icing in the centre of the flower and 'pull' it to make a longish stamen.

When it is dry paint it yellow-orange. Paint a tiny leaf-green calyx on the outside of the flower.

Tuberose

*M*ost brides like to have a tuberose in their bouquet so why not on the cake? This is not a 'filler' flower. It is large enough for one flower and one bud to make a spray. The flower can be made in white paste and coloured later, or in cream-coloured paste.

Flowers

1. Shape a long bud of paste on the end of a knotted/hooked piece of wire and make firm.
2. Hollow out a 90mm long cone with a hair-roller pin making the cavity wide enough to take another row of petals and the bud.
3. Make five long cuts around the rim to make five petals, mitre each one, flatten, and gently curve outwards.
4. Make a second but slightly smaller cone (65mm) and make five petals in the same way. Cut off the base of the cone and fit it into the first cone, wetting the back of the petals and arranging them alternatively with those of the first cone.

5. Insert the wired bud and gently mould the whole flower into shape. Cut off any excess paste at the base of the first flower and neaten on to the wire. Leave to dry.

Buds

Mould a long bulbous heavy bud of paste on to the end of a hooked piece of wire.

Colour the flower dark cream with liquid colour or chalk, starting at the centre and paling to light cream at the edges of the petals. Colour the buds cream with brownish-pink tips.

Little mint ladies

*T*hese little flowers are like an open bell; they have wide petals and a striated or spotted throat. The red, purple, lilac, mauve, pink, greenish-yellow, cream and white of their colouring make them very useful as a spray flower or for use with orchids.

Method

Basic bell

1. Hollow out a 2cm cone of paste with a No. 2 former tool and ease out the bottom half so that the bell-shape is formed
2. Make three long cuts in the lower half of the rim to make three petals.
3. Make two long cuts in the lower rim to make two petals.
4. Round the top of the lower petals and gently elongate and flatten the whole petal.
5. Mitre the top petals, flatten the whole petal and gently roll the top outwards.
6. Reshape the bell with a No. 4 former tool.
7. Flute the bottom petals outwards, using a round toothpick.

Variations

Peppermint lady:
Make as for basic bell and allow to dry. Colour the centre with yellow chalk. Using a non-toxic colouring pen mark tiny rows of grape-violet dots from the centre of the flower over the top petals.

Blue mist lady:
Make as for the basic bell but with three, not

two, cuts in the lower rim of the cone. Round and flatten the petals so that they nearly come together. Mix some violet colour with a touch of blue with pure alcohol and paint first the back of the flower and then the front. Use deep purple chalk to colour the centre.

Mountain mist lady:
Make the basic bell but roll the top petals inwards so that they face each other. Cut the lower rim of the cone so that it has two narrow petals on each side of a wider one. Indent the bottom centre of the wide one and, using a round toothpick, roll it backwards. Cut the two narrow petals to about half-length, flatten gently and ease out sideways.

Colour the centre of the flower with mauve chalk; dot the bottom petals with a non-toxic tangerine colouring pen with the dots going down into the bell, then put two small tangerine stripes on the side petals.

Silver mint lady:
Make the bell with all the petals facing inward. Roll the three bottom ones upward, using a round toothpick. Paint the centre of the flower with yellow chalk bringing the colour on to the centre bottom petal. Mix some pink-mauve colour with pure alcohol and first paint the back of the flower then the front. Go over the lower edges of the petals a second time.

Chinese mint lady:
Make the basic bell, but with the petals all the same size. Round the tops and ball each petal from the back. Reform the centre of the flower with a ball tool. Paint the petals all over with pink paint mixed with pure alcohol.

Each flower should be wired. Three to six are needed to make a spray.

Daffodil

*T*hese flowers must be made from paste
rolled as thinly as possible otherwise they
will look ugly and bulky. They can be made in
white paste and coloured when dry or in paste
to which lemon colouring with a touch of
orange has been added.

Method

1. Using a daffodil cutter cut three petals and
   'finger' the edges.

2. Roll each one out, lengthwise first, then
   crosswise.
3. Press crepe paper on to the petals so that
   the indentations of the paper give the paste
   a natural look.
4. Using a container as described for
   carnations arrange the three petals in the
   container and ease the centre down with a
   No. 2 former tool.

5. Cut a second set of three petals and repeat
   2 and 3.
6. Place alternately inside the first row of
   petals which are in the holder. Leave to dry.

Trumpet

1. Make a cone of paste approximately ⅔ the
   size of the finished flower. You know what a
   daffodil looks like.

2. Pinch out the top edges of the cone and
   finger-flute or flute with a round-headed
   toothpick.

3. Insert the bottom of a No. 3 former tool into the cone and open it up into a bell-shaped trumpet.

4. Wet the bottom of the trumpet with water and place it in the centre of the petals in the container.
5. Fix three or four yellow stamens into place using a dab of royal icing.

Calyx

Make a calyx of five sepals from paste coloured pale green. Wire it. Wax the cup of the calyx and insert the dried flower.

Sweetheart rose

*T*he subtle colouring of the petals makes this rose particularly interesting.
You will need white, pink and yellow paste. The petals in the outer row are white, the second row petals are yellow and white, the third are pink and white and the centre ones are pink and yellow.

To get the delicate colour combination take a small ball of white paste and an equally sized one of yellow and wedge them together; rub gently to combine the colours until the white is at the top of the petal and the other at the bottom with no clean line where the colours join. Do the same with white and pink paste and pink and yellow paste. You will need approximately 7 to 8 petals to form the outer row of the flower. Use as many other petals as necessary to fill-in the flower.

I make this flower on a ring so that the outer petals are supported, otherwise it can look flat and uninteresting.

Method

1. Roll a piece of paste about the size of a 20 cent coin and 3mm thick and shape it into a ring. Allow to dry thoroughly.

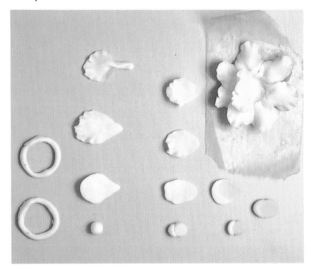

2. The petals are tear-drop shaped and about 2cm long and 60mm wide. Finger-flute the top edges and pleat the bottom.

3. Place the ring on a square of waxed paper and arrange the outer row of white petals. Each petal is attached to the paper with a small drop of water. Each petal folds over the ring and overlaps the previous one. Flatten the base of the petals so that the central area is as open as possible and leaves room for the inner rows of petals. You can support the white petals by little pads of waxed paper to help keep the shape.

4. Insert the white and yellow petals, keeping the yellow at the base. Cup them so that they stand up all round and ease them back over the first row.

5. Insert the white and pink petals inside the second row, with the pink portion to the base. Keep them standing up all round.

6. Fill the centre of the flower with the pink and yellow petals, either colour can be at the top.

Abelia

*T*he small flower can be used on its own or in a cluster. The pale mauve bell has a tiny pale-cinnamon coloured calyx, the leaves are multi-coloured.

Flowers

1. Make a 90mm long cone from a piece of white paste.

2. Hollow out with a hair-roller pin and make five short cuts around the rim to make five petals.

3. Trim around the top of the petals. Flatten them gently.

4. Using the ball-tool enlarge the hollowed base of the cone to make it bell-shaped.

5. Run the ball-tool up the back of each petal and curve the edges outwards.
6. Insert wire in the flower.
7. Using the palest mauve colour (it must not be violet) mixed with pure alcohol, paint the back of the flower, deepening the tone slightly down one side toward the bottom. Leave to dry.
8. Using a tiny blossom cutter, cut a calyx from cinnamon-coloured paste and attach to the flower with a touch of water.
9. Put a small spot of royal icing into the throat of the bell and insert four stamens allowing them to protrude slightly from the bell.

Buds

Mould a small piece of paste on to the end of the wire to make a small bulbous bud. Paint a darker shade of mauve than the flower.

Leaves

Make a small oval pointed leaf in green paste and splash with russety-brown water colours. Insert wire.

To assemble

The darker coloured buds must complement the flower, not dominate the spray.

Tiger lily

*I*f you follow the instructions you can make any member of the *lilium* family, just vary the colouring as needed. Work in white paste and colour the parts when dry. Make one petal at a time and dry each one separately.

Tiger lilies have six hammer-head stamens and one other with a knob end.

Method

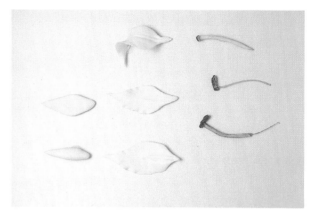

1. Using beans of modelling paste shape six petals approximately 7.5cm long with a softly pointed top and a long tapering 'tail'.
2. Flatten each petal.
3. Curve and twist the pulled out tail just a little.
4. Widen each petal from the base to half-way up.
5. Flute each side of the upper part of the petals.
6. Using a knife, make a gentle depression in the centre of each petal from the base to three quarters of the way up.

7. Cut out a circle of aluminium foil and insert it into an egg-cup pressing it down to the base and against the sides and

smoothing the surplus at the rim out into a circle.

8. Place each petal in the egg-cup in the following order.
   - petal one at 12 o'clock
   - petal two at 7 o'clock
   - petal three at 5 o'clock
   - petal four at 2 o'clock
   - petal five at 6 o'clock
   - petal six at 10 o'clock

   While placing the petals in position, shape and twist them back a little making sure you leave the centre open and deep enough to take six stamens and one anther. **Do not allow the petals to touch one another.** Leave to dry with the foil providing a support for the petals.

9. Colour each petal separately. For an orange tiger lily — mix orange colour with pure alcohol and wash all over back and front of the petal and allow to dry thoroughly. Using a darker shade of orange make a wash down the centre of each petal. Allow to dry. The markings on the throat of the petals can be made in two different ways:

   Using a fine paint brush, you can make tiny dots of a darker shade of orange, and with a half-dry brush, smudge them into the colour of the petal,

   Or

   You can pipe many tiny dots of royal icing on to the petal and paint them a dark orange when the icing is dry.

   The lily in the photographs was coloured with a wash of orange and a touch of peach mixed with pure alcohol.

Stamens

These must be very well-made. You can use wire with a small head of paste or make them from paste. Roll the paste as thin as a round toothpick. Form the hammer head by lapping back half the paste at the top, flattening it and then shaping it into a curve. Dry flat. The anther is straighter and longer with a flat knobbed top. Paint and dry the stamens and anther then insert in the flower carefully using a little royal icing to hold them in place.

Crab apple

*T*he unusual burgundy colouring of this flower ranges from dark buds and small flowers to very pale larger flowers. It is important to note that the flowers are white on the inside and are only coloured on the underside

Method

1. Make a 60cm long bean of white paste and flatten it, keeping the point to the base.

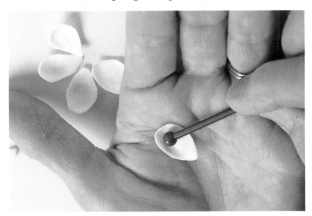

2. Cup the edges gently and leave the petal to dry.
3. Make five of these petals for each flower.
4. Place a small dob of royal icing on to a small square of wax paper.
5. Place the five petals into the royal icing just overlapping each one at the point. Make some flowers with petals half-closed and others gradually opening to the fully opened flower. Allow to dry.

6. Fill the centres with half-headed cream stamens.
7. Make bulbous buds held in place with royal icing of varying sizes. Wire and dry.

8. When the buds and flowers are dry paint with non-toxic chalk or petal dust. Match the right colour from a real flower.
9. Make an oval leaf approximately 1.25cm long just like a sweet apple leaf. Finely serrate the edges and dry fairly flat. Colour a pale apple-green. Use plenty of buds when making the spray.

Fuchsia

*F*uchsias are not the easiest flowers to make and the paste must be handled lightly. Their strong natural colours can be a bit heavy, so create a paler colour theme of your own. Make them in white paste and colour later.

Method — large single fuchsia

1. Wire six stamens together and cover the wire twist with a tiny strip of Stemtex.
2. Make a small Dainty Bess-shaped petal and cup it quite deeply.
3. Make three more petals.

4. Moisten each one about half-way up from the pointed end and join together, overlapping slightly.

5. Wet the back of the first petal and bring the fourth petal around to form a bell and press gently together.
6. Pull the wired stamens through and neaten the bottom of the bell on to the wire. Leave to dry.
7. Hollow out a 2cm cone of paste and make four long cuts into the rim to make four sepals.
8. Mitre each one into a neat leaf shape.

9. Slip the shaped cone up the wire and

attach it to the back of the bell with a dob of water. Neaten it on to the wire.
10. Shape the paste to make a bell shape when the calyx fits on to the wire.
11. Using one colour for the bell and a deeper or paler shade of the same colour for the calyx, paint the flower. The small bud ending of the calyx which fits on to the wire should be pale green.

Method — double fuchsia

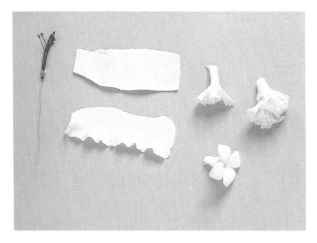

1. Wire six stamens together and cover the wire twist with a tiny strip of Stemtex.
2. Roll out a piece of white modelling paste approximately 5cm x 2.5cm as thinly as possible.

3. Flute one long edge and then concertina the petal, using a little water to hold the folds in place.
4. Using a second piece of paste make an identical petal.

5. With water join the two petals together down the long edge and shape into a bell.
6. Insert the wired stamens into the bell, neaten the back and leave the flower to dry.
7. Hollow out a 2.5cm cone of paste and make four long cuts in the rim to make four petals.
8. Mitre the corners of each one and broaden the centre by flattening and turning back the edges.

2. Hollow out a 9mm long cone of white modelling paste with a toothpick.
3. Make four long cuts into the rim to make four petals.
4. Round and slightly flatten each petal.

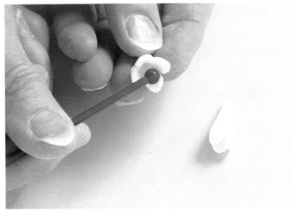

9. Insert wire holding the first set of petals into this flower-shape, pull the shape up the wire and neaten on to the back of the bell.
10. Squeeze the junction very gently and mark with a knife to make a small bulbous ending to the flower.
11. Paint the flower pale mauve or pink. Paint the outer rim of petals a darker shade of the same colour and the small bulbous ending a pale green. All the colours should be mixed with pure alcohol. The wire should be green.

Method — tiny single fuchsia

1. Wire four stamens and cover wire twist with a small strip of Stemtex.

5. Use a No.2 ball-tool to bell out each petal by rolling lengthwise and sideways.
6. Make a bell from the four petals by overlapping each one keeping the bell long and fairly tightly closed.
7. Pull the stamens on to the wire through the bell.

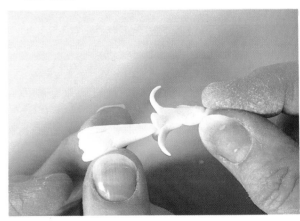

8. Cut a four-petal calyx as for the other two fuchsias but make the petals longer

and thinner. Insert the wire and draw up to the tiny bell. Pinch gently to make a bulbous ending.

9. Colour, using a lighter and darker shade for petals and calyx.

Daphne

$\mathcal{T}$his lovely old flower makes me remember my grandmother so I feel it is just right for a cake for our older ladies. I pulled the real flower to pieces many times before I found the right way to make it. The flowers in each head open at different times so you can make your own decision about the number of buds, half-opened flowers and fully-opened flowers to use in each head. I use a pale burgundy-pink paste and make about 20 buds, from the very tiniest to the half-open, two half-opened flowers and four or five fully-opened flowers.

Flowers

1. Hollow out a 60cm cone of paste and keep the tail of the cone long.

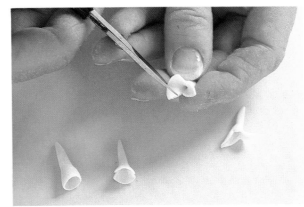

2. Make two long cuts in the rim to form two petals facing each other — petals one and two.
3. Cut two leaf-shaped petals with a pointed tip and, with water, attach each one between the petals at the side and using a round toothpick, gently roll them backwards, leaving the first two petals upright. Call these petals three and four.
4. Insert a yellow-headed stamen in the centre of the flower and hold in position with a tiny dob of royal icing.
5. Mix some burgundy-pink colour and a touch of mauve in a little water and lightly edge petals one and two with very little colour, then paint petals three and four all over the back and tail.

Buds

1. Make a long bean of paste with a thicker head. You will be making many buds so vary the size of the heads but always keep a long tail. To make half a bud, flag out the top and wrap it around the bud.
2. Paint the bud burgundy leaving a tiny amount of paste showing at the tip to represent the unopened flower.

Calyx

1. Hollow out a 2.5cm long cone of green paste and widen the rim until it is about 2cm in diameter.
2. Make short cuts around the rim and mitre the sepals.
3. While paste is still wet — half-fill the calyx with royal icing and fill with buds, half-opened buds and lastly, flowers, tightening the calyx at the back but leaving enough to hold the head together. Leave to dry.

Leaves

Make the leaves in leaf-green paste and paint in the same colour when dry. If you cannot use the real leaf cut a leaf shape with a point at both ends and wide in its centre mark.

A spray of three heads with accompanying leaves is sufficient for a large cone.

Gardenia

The paste for this beautiful white flower must be as fine as possible and it is not easy to make. When the real flower opens, the outer two rows of petals flatten and curve downwards and the other petals open at different stages, so when you shape the flower, bear this in mind.

Method

1. Make a ring of white paste about the size of a 20 cent coin and 30mm thick. Dampen

one end and attach to the other. Leave to dry thoroughly on a square of waxed paper.
2. Make a Dainty Bess-shaped petal. Slightly ease the sides and bring the top up to a gentle peak. Press on to a pad of crepe paper to give the petal texture. Make approximately eight petals.
3. Dampen the paper in the centre of the ring of paste. With a ball-tool, arrange petals around it, tail downwards and overlapping slightly until you have formed the outer ring of the flower. Do not allow petals to lie

flat. Support with waxed paper and ease into shape.

4. Make a second inner row of petals and if they need support use waxed paper again.
5. Continue making rows of petals allowing them to stand up more towards the centre.
6. Leave the centre open enough to place three small yellow boomerang-shaped pieces into it.

Leaves

1. If possible cut the oval shape from the real flower.
2. Cut the shape and finger gently.

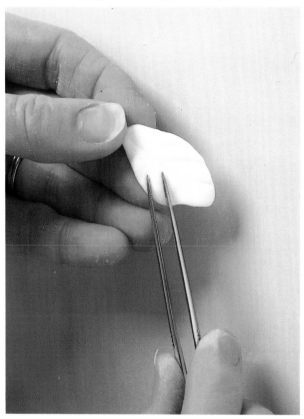

3. Mark the centre vein with the back of a knife.
4. Put in the side markings with tweezers.
5. Mix leaf green and yellow paint and add a touch of brown. Paint dry leaves.
6. When completely dry rub leaves with a speck of petroleum jelly (which is quite safe) to give them a dull shine.

Buds

1. These are very special and must be copied from the real thing, but they do finish a spray. Make a 2.5cm long bean of paste

with a point at both ends .
2. Place tiny rolled pieces of paste at the base of the cone letting them stand out to form a calyx.
3. Paint the same green as the leaves.

Stephanotis

*T*his lively flower makes an excellent decoration for a wedding cake. Make it in white modelling paste and dust the dry flower with yellow chalk to give it a soft creamy look.

Method

1. Hollow out a 2cm long cone of white modelling paste.
2. Make five short cuts around the rim to create five equally-sized petals.
3. Round the edges of the petals.
4. Insert a ball-tool into the cone right down to the bottom and gently shape the paste

with it. Remove the tool and roll the centre part of the cone between your fingers. This will leave the petals at the top of the cone, a narrow section in the middle and a bulb shape at the bottom.

5. Turn the flower over and gently 'ball' the back of each petal. Turn back again and gently twist one or two of the petals.
6. Use a knotted wire to wire each flower.
7. Dust the back of the flower with yellow chalk.

Bud

The bud has the same narrow middle section as the flower. Mix cream colour with a touch of orange colour and pure alcohol. Paint down from the top getting lighter twoards the base.

Calyx

Cut a very tiny calyx with the smaller forget-me-not cutter. Slip it up the wire and attach to the back of the flower with water.

Leaves

Cut dark-green paste leaves. Round leaves at the top end and deeply vein. Paint with the same dark-green colour.

As a filler three flowers and three buds will do. If used as a spray on its own make any number of both.

Black-eyed Susan

*T*he bright colour of the flowers and the unusual shape of the buds make this a very effective cake decoration.

Flower

1. Make a cone of modelling paste 2.5cm long with a diameter of 1.25cm at the rim end.
2. Using a No. 3 former, hollow out the cone until the diameter of the opened rim is about 2.5cm.
3. Make five short cuts around the rim to create five petals.
4. Round the corners and then flatten each petal.

5. Immediately press petals into a pad of crepe paper to give natural texture.
6. Join tip of left thumb and forefinger together to make a circle and drop the cone into it, pointed side down, with the petals lying out flat from the centre.
7. With the right hand gently press and extend the bottom part of the cone to form a long thin tail, while gently squeezing the circle of thumb and forefinger so that the centre of the flower narrows to a 9cm diameter throat.
8. Insert a No.1 former into the centre of the flower and gently hollow it out.

Colour

1. Mix orange colour with a touch of apricot or peach with pure alcohol.
2. Paint front and back of petals.
3. Paint tail of flower with mauve colour mixed with pure alcohol.
4. When flower is completely dry, paint the centre of the flower — the 'black eye' — with deep purple straight from the bottle. It is essential that this colour should not run. The 'eye' should be in sharp contrast to the colour of the petals.

Buds

1. Make a cone of green paste and flatten the rim end into a square.
2. Invert it so that it stands on the square base.
3. Using a sharp knife make a cut from the pointed end to two-thirds the way down.
4. Open cut slightly and insert a hair-roller pin to keep it open.

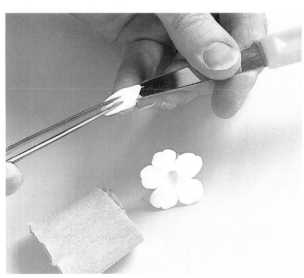

5. Using tweezers pinch a vertical ridge on each side.
6. Take the pin out and replace with a knife. While keeping the cut open you can now work on the flat areas supported by the knife.
7. With the tweezers make a vertical ridge down the centre of each side from the point of the cone to the wide base.

Leaves

I pressed a real leaf into thinly-rolled out

modelling paste and cut it out. When it was dry I painted it with a mixture of leaf-green and yellow straight from the bottle.

To assemble

To use on its own, make vine stems by rolling thinly and colouring the same as the leaves. Arrange and place leaves in groups with buds and scattered flowers. If you are using it as a filler, two flowers, one bud and two leaves would be sufficient.

Azaleas

*T*his is a very handy flower. It is easy to make, and comes in many different colours and in white with a rim of colour around the petals. Four of the petals are the same size, the fifth is slightly wider. I dry and form these in a cup of alfoil held in a plasticine holder.

Method

1. Using white paste or pale-coloured paste make a bean 2.5cm long, rounded at the top and pointed at the bottom.
2. Flatten, thin out finely and gently round the top into a point by easing it between your fingers.

3. Place the petal in the holder and ease it backwards with a ball-tool.
4. Make the second petal and place next to the first one, just overlapping at the bottom.
5. Make petals three and four and mark them down the centre with the back of a knife to cup them a little.
6. Place these two petals into the holder, one facing 3 o'clock and the other facing 9 o'clock, with the pointed ends facing down into the holder.

7. Make the fifth petal wider and mark down the centre with a ball-tool.

8. Place it in the holder facing 6 o'clock with its tail covering the tails of the other petals in the throat of the flower.

9. Take the flower in the alfoil out of the holder and gently squeeze the back of it, closing up the centre around the straight end of a ball-tool, but leaving just enough room to take a small dob of royal icing to hold the stamens. Allow to dry.
10. For white paste, paint the flower all over with colour mixed with pure alcohol then allow it to dry thoroughly before painting in the dots of colour in the throat. Give another wash of colour all over to matt the dots. For pale-coloured paste, just paint in the details.
11. When flower is dry use a dob of royal icing to fix five stamens with small heads and a larger one with a larger head in the throat of the flower. The colour of the stamens should match the flower.

Primrose

*T*he five pale yellow petals each have a cleft in the centre and a tiny orange triangle at the base, pointing towards the centre. This triangle makes the 'eye' of the flower.

Method

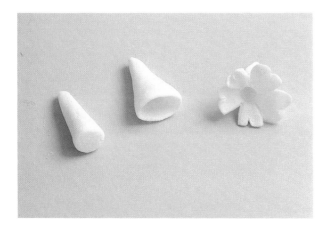

1. Hollow out a 3cm long cone of white paste to one-third of the way down and make the rim about 1.25cm in diameter.
2. Make five short cuts around the rim to create five equal-sized petals and then open the flower out a little.
3. Round the petal corners and make a shallow cut in the centre of the top of each one. Flatten out each petal to make it heart-shaped.
4. Wire the bell. Do not smooth the paste down on the wire.

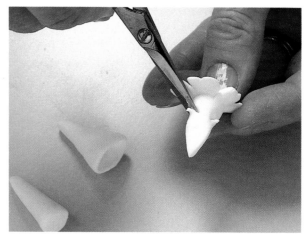

5. Turn the flower upside down and make three snips into the thickness of the paste about half-way down the bell. Ease the snipped paste out and shape to make a calyx. Firm it on to the wire.
6. Mix some egg-yellow paint, a touch of orange and lemon-yellow with pure alcohol and paint the back of the flower. Paint the front. Leave to dry.
7. When thoroughly dry paint a tiny orange triangle across the base of each petal with the point of the triangle facing into the centre. The triangle should not be more than one-quarter the length of the petal.
8. Paint the calyx pale green.
9. Put a very small dob of royal icing deep into the throat of the flower and insert about five cream-coloured stamens.

Pansy

*M*aking this pretty flower is reasonably easy, but colouring it is not. It is a good idea to study the real flower. The five petals can be made and dried separately or made and placed wet into the dry calyx. I prefer to make them separately, and then assemble them. The petals are arranged in two pairs and one

base petal. Depending on your choice the shape is that of a Dainty Bess from 5 cent size up to 10 cent size.

Method

1. For the two top petals make two Dainty Bess petals, cup and flute them slightly and dry flat with their points just overlapping.
2. Make the two side petals the same shape and when cupping them in the palm of your hand place the point facing across the palm. Flute slightly, and dry flat.
3. Make the base petal a Dainty Bess shape but pull the width to either side, leaving the point in the centre. Cup and flute. Dry flat.
4. The points of each petal form the centre face of the pansy.

Colour

1. Wash over all the petals in a basic pale colour and allow to dry thoroughly.
2. Paint in the palest shade colour furthest from the centre. This allows the colour to deepen as you reach the centre point.
3. When you paint a dark colour onto the petal, wash the brush, damp dry and with a push-pull movement where the colours meet, smudge the two colours together.
4. Each colour added must shade and smudge into the one before. Do not have defined edges between the colours.
5. If you use black to darken the centre area be careful. Better to use the black non-toxic felt pens.

Assembly

1. Place a dob of royal icing onto a square of waxed paper.
2. Take the top two petals and place the points just overlapping into the royal icing.
3. Next, place the two side petals in with their points touching at the centre.
4. Lastly, place in the base petal making sure its point fits up into the tiny space between the two side ones.
5. When dry, pipe a very tiny horseshoe in the centre covering all the points of the five petals. When this is dry paint it a soft yellow.

To wire a pansy

Attach a wet-wired calyx to a dry-assembled flower.

Leaves

These are long and flat with rounded indentations and are a lightish leaf-green colour.

Cattleya orchid

*O*rchids are heavy flowers and must be made well. Cattleya is one of the softer ones and looks very pleasing providing the fluting of the two wing petals and that of the lip is well done and the paste is as fine as possible. They are usually used as the main flower and are suitable for any kind of cake. If they are to be the theme on a wedding cake, use two on the bottom layer and three on the top tier. Soften with fillers and tulle.

Method

1. Make three long finger-shaped sepals about 5cm long in white modelling paste. Curve them backwards. They will sit one each side of the lip and one up the centre back.

2. Make two wing petals the shape of a large Dainty Bess petal but longer. With the back of a knife mark a centre vein the full length of the back of the petal and turn the centre up to the point. Flute the edges with a round toothpick.

3. While wet, turn the petal over, and holding

it in the palm of your left hand run a ball-tool up and down each side of the centre mark, thus cupping out the front of the petals.

4. Turn back over and dry with a slight backward curve.

Lip

1. Hollow out a 2.5cm long cone and extend the bottom half of the cone by gently pulling down.
2. Cut the top edge in two halves and round the cut edges.
3. Fine out the lower half of the cone with your fingers and cut a 9cm 'V' into this lower edge. Slightly round the corners of the V.
4. Flute with a rounded toothpick right around both edges from the top cut to the bottom and make them as fluted as possible.
5. Reshape the throat of the lip with a No. 3 former and dry, allowing the lower edge to come to the front.
6. Spray the three sepals and the two wing petals with a soft-pink colour mixed with pure alcohol. Allow to dry.
7. Yellow chalk the throat of the lip, bringing the colour out about half-way. Brush a dark-pink chalk over the rest of the lip right out to the edges. Dust all around the two wing petal edges with darker pink. The flower can be left white with just a yellow-throated lip. There are many more colours in this species.
8. Put a drop of royal icing on to a square of waxed paper. Place the lip in the centre with a front sepal on each side. Allow to set for about two minutes. Place wing petals

behind and to the side of the front sepals. Support them from the back with cotton wool balls and allow to set for two minutes. Set in the back petal, standing up. Support and leave flower to dry.

Clematis

*T*his flower fascinates me because of the softness of the colourings and the starkness of the black eye and black stamens. There are eight petals, all the same size and shape. They are only slightly curved and I found the curved patty tins excellent for drying them in.

Method

1. Mould a 2.5cm long bean in white modelling paste with a point at both ends. Flatten then widen the middle section.
2. Place on the work board and gently roll out as thinly as possible.
3. Cut to an oval-leaf shape, keeping a very thin point at the top end.

4. Mark with the back of a knife from the bottom point half-way up the centre. Fan out the marks each side of this centre one shortening them as you near the side edge.

5. Press the front side of the petal into a pad of crepe paper to give it texture.
6. Gently flute one spot on either side of the top half of the petal.
7. Dry in the patty tins.
8. Make eight petals for each flower.
9. When completely dry, paint the back of the petal and then the front with a pale colour mixed with pure alcohol. Allow to dry. Some of these flowers have a darker splash of colour up the centre of each petal.

Assembly

The petals fit together in an unusual way, so use the clock face for reference. Place a dob of royal icing on a square of waxed paper and position the petals in this order:
• petal one at 2 o'clock
• petal two at 10 o'clock
• petal three at 5 o'clock
• petal four a 7 o'clock
• petal five at 3 o'clock
• petal six at 9 o'clock

• petal seven under numbers three and four
• petal eight on top of numbers one and two and at 12 o'clock
With a clean brush, work the remaining royal icing up to a raised centre peak, leaving enough icing around the peak to take in short pieces of black cotton to make stamens. When this is very dry, paint the area of royal icing around the cotton a pale yellow, then paint the peak black leaving the tiniest white spot in the centre.

Quick and easy orchid

*I*f you have a rush job, a flower that will cover a fair area is very handy. Having this in mind I created this little orchid. The petals were cut with the middle-size frangipani cutter, and I used a little mint lady for the lip. If it is not big enough a larger cutter can be used and the lip made from a larger mint lady. The colouring was taken from the Cattleya orchid.

Method

1. Cut five petals with the frangipani cutter

and on four of them trim the rounded end to a point.

2. With a knife make five markings, in a fan shape, from the point to half-way up each petal.

3. Twist two petals slightly and dry flat (side petals).

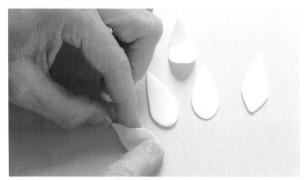

4. Curve two into a crescent and set them on their sides to dry (upper-side petals).

5. Shape the rounded fifth petal into a crescent and set on its side to dry (centre-back petal). This petal has a wider space to fill.

6. Make a peppermint lady but do not cut the bottom section into three segments. Leave in one piece and roll well with a round toothpick. Recup the throat with a No. 2 former tool and allow to dry.

7. Colour the base of each petal with a yellow paint mixed with pure alcohol. When half-dry paint the back and then the front with peach colour mixed with pure alcohol, taking in the edge of the yellow.

8. When dry, dust rust-coloured chalk lightly up the centre of each petal.

9. Colour the lip-throat with yellow chalk. Paint the back and front of the lip with lemon-yellow liquid straight from the bottle. When dry dust the whole edge of the lip with a deeper-pink chalk — make the edging about 3cm.

Assembly

Put a dob of royal icing on to a square of waxed paper. Set the two side petals into the icing facing the front. Leave enough room for the lip. Set the lip. Leave to dry and later put in the two upper side petals and support them from the back with a cotton wool ball. Allow to set a little. Using a small amount of royal icing at the back of the throat set in the back centre petal. Support it with cotton wool balls until it is dry and firm.

Japonica

*T*he first of the spring flowers, the flowering quince, as the japonica is commonly known, has flowers of glowing red which contrast beautifully with the dark-green leaves. It makes a lovely decoration for a fortieth (ruby) anniversary cake.

Calyx

1. Hollow out a 1cm long cone of white paste and make five cuts into the rim to make equally-sized sepals.

2. Mitre sepals to a long point, flatten and slightly cup each one.
3. Attach to a hooked wire and allow to dry.
4. Paint dark green.

Flower

1. Make five Dainty Bess petals in white paste about the size of a five cent coin. Cup each one slightly, gently flute the top edge and leave to dry.
2. Paint back and front of the petals with a mixture of scarlet with a touch of rouge. The colours can be used straight from the bottle.
3. Using a little royal icing to hold them in place, put the five dry and painted petals into the dry calyx just overlapping each preceeding one at the point.
4. Fill the centre of the flower with tiny yellow stamen, threads made as finely as possible, and when they are dry tip each one with brown.

5. Make a medium-size bud, paint it red, and then paint a dark-green calyx. The wires holding the flowers and the buds should be painted the same green as the calyx.

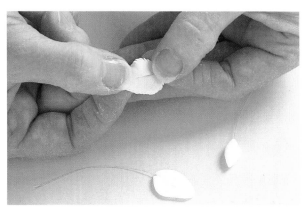

6. To make a leaf, roll a bean of paste about 60mm long and push a single wire right up the middle of it. Flatten as finely as possible, cut to the shape of a rose leaf, serrate the edges and mark the veins. Slightly bend the wire in the leaf. Allow to dry and paint in the same dark green as the calyx.

Kurrajong

*T*he flowers of this native tree are either red and white, yellow and orange, or white with red spots. The strong colours make them very useful as decorations for a cake made with a man in mind.

Method

1. Hollow out a 1.25cm long cone of white modelling paste with a hair-roller pin. Widen the rim.

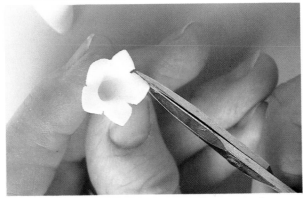

2. Make five short cuts, equally spaced apart around the rim.

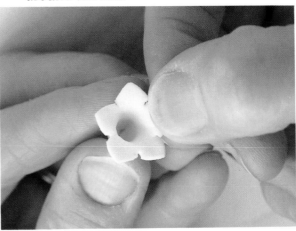

3. Neatly mitre the top of each of the five petals and flatten them gently.

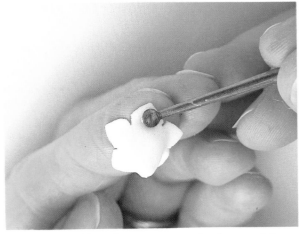

4. Use a ball-tool to open up the base of the flower and make a shallow bell.
5. Insert knotted wire.
6. Turn flower over and using the tool, 'ball' each petal from the back.
7. Turn flower right-side up and arrange the petals so that they stand at a 90 degree angle from the rim.
8. Paint the back of the flower scarlet or pillar-box red with colour straight from the bottle. Don't let the paint colour the front. Allow to dry.
9. Mix some red and orange chalk and paint the throat of the flower from the bottom up to where it begins to 'bell'.
10. Insert two or three red or yellow stamen with a dab of royal icing to secure them.

Note

If you are making a white flower just paint red dots on the back of the ball, and a deeper yellow on the throat.

Buds

1. Wrap a piece of paste about two-thirds the length of the flower around the hooked end of a piece of wire and firm it into place.
2. Shape the head and make it bulbous. Mark it to show five closed petals. Paint the bud red, leaving a little white at the tip.

Boronia

*T*here are many varieties of boronia. I find the brown and pink the easiest to make, their colours blend beautifully with wild flower arrangements.

Brown boronia method

1. Hollow out a 60mm long cone of yellow modelling paste.
2. Make four short cuts an equal distance apart around the rim to create four petals.

3. Round the top of each petal and, using the small ball-tool, cup each petal gently.
4. Insert a knotted wire into the flower.

5. Ball-tool the centre of the flower, bringing up all four petals to form a cup. Allow to dry.

6. Paint the outside of the flower chestnut-brown with paint straight from the bottle mixed with pure alcohol. Do not forget the edges.

Pink boronia method

1. Hollow out a 90mm long cone of pale burgundy-pink modelling paste.

2. Make four or five short cuts an equal distance apart around the rim of the petal. Some flowers can have four petals, some five.
3. Mitre each petal to a gentle point and flatten gently.
4. Wire the flower and reform the centre, cupping it a little. Allow to dry.
5. If you wish, you can insert one dark stamen held in place with a tiny dot of royal icing.
6. Paint the back of the flower with burgundy-pink paint straight from the bottle. Do not forget the edges.

Buds

Brown boronia buds are short and bulborous. Pink boronia buds are long, thin and pointed. Three flowers and a bud make a small spray.

Christmas bells

$\mathcal{T}$hese beautiful flowers have details I missed for many years — for instance, the tiny speck of green on the tip of each petal point. I suggest you study the real flower or a clear photograph of one.

Method

1. Make a cone of pale yellow modelling paste approximately two-thirds the size of the finished flower.

2. Hollow out the centre of the cone using a hair-roller pin and roll it gently twice, then ease the cone up on the pin and lengthen it to a bell shape of the required depth. Do not let it spread out too much.

3. Make two short cuts around the rim to divide it into half.
4. Make three short cuts in each half. You now have six petals of equal size.

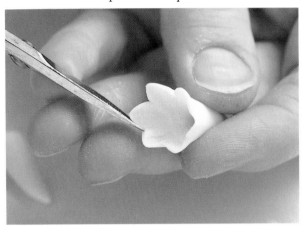

5. Make the petals into a curve.

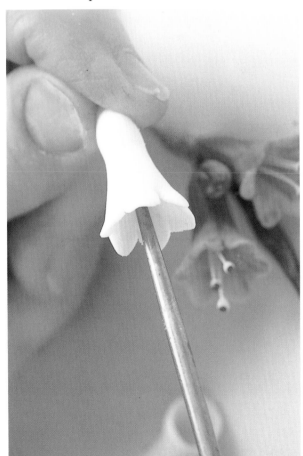

6. Place each petal in turn along the under finger and gently insert the ball-end of the hair roller and deepen the throat into a bell shape.
7. Wire the flower, keeping the knotted end of the wire hidden deep in the bell. Allow to dry.

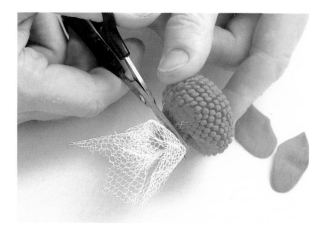

8. Mix a little orange paint with water and paint both the inside and the outside of the bell. While the colour is still damp but not wet dab a spot of scarlet or pillar-box red on the outside of the flower where the wire joins the bell and gently move it upwards, leaving an orange margin. The colours should merge gently, there should be no hard edges. Paint a tiny spot of green on the outside of the tip of each flower. Paint a tiny pale-green calyx in each bell.

Leaves

Shape a small bean of paste into a long thin, smooth slightly curved leaf. To make a spray use two or three flowers with a bud.

Waratah

There are two ways to make these flowers, one is very quick and easy, and the other takes time and effort but produces a far better looking flower.

If the flower is needed for the side of a small cake the quick method would be fine. But if the spray is going to be the main theme on the top of the cake or on a plaque, more detail and care is needed. Always use modelling paste coloured with pillar-box-red food colouring powder, and make sure it is well worked through the paste. To make this flower in white paste and paint it afterwards is a waste of time and an unnecessary test of patience.

Method 1 — quick and easy

1. Take a ball of red paste about the size of a 50 cent coin, making sure it is smooth,

then cover it with a good sized square of large-holed nylon net.
2. Gather the net round the ball and twist it so tight that the paste is pushed through the holes in the net.
3. Squeeze until the tracts are long enough (don't squeeze till the paste falls out of the net).
4. Tighten net under the ball and cut off the excess.
5. Set ball down carefully and allow to dry.
6. Make about 10 leaf-shape outer petals one at a time.
7. Arrange them around the ball setting one lot up and around the centre.
8. Place the outer row out from these, making sure that they do not make the flower look like a star fish. Some cup slightly upwards.

Method 2 — time and effort

1. Working in the red paste make about 20 comma shaped pieces in six different sizes. Roll a small piece of paste between your fingers, leaving one end with a head and the other end with a sharp point.
2. Curve the commas around your finger tip

to form the shape. Lay out in rows and allow to dry. Make the last two rows with longer tails.

3. When the tails of these are dry make a tiny petal and wrap around the comma from the inside curve to the outside.

4. Allow them all to dry thoroughly. Keep the longer and tailed commas with the petals attached on one side.

Assembly

1. Take a ball of red fondant about the size of a 50 cent coin. Pierce three holes into the base and allow to dry.

2. Shape into a blunt-ended dome slightly tapered at both ends.

3. Start at the top, making sure the first circle covers the top of the ball, push the commas into the wet ball, point end in the curve nestling on to the ball.

4. Moving down the cone place the comma heads between or close up to the one above.

5. For the last row at the base of the cone use the longer-tailed commas with the little petals.

6. Poke a round toothpick up into the centre of the ball from beneath. This will form a stem to make handling easier when the paste has dried.

7. To dry, place a square of waxed paper into the concave area of the wooden drying rack and pass the toothpick through and allow the flower to nestle in and dry.

8. Make leaf-shaped red petals as fine as possible. Take a bean 1.25cm long and finger it out keeping a point at one end. Extend to an even finer point and gently pinch. Widen the petal in the middle and leave a blunt end at the other end.

Now place the hair-roller pin down the length of the petal and gently roll it from side to side. This slightly curves up the petal. Place these petals up and around the base of the centre onto the commas. Stand the second row out from the first making sure it does not have a star effect. The toothpick helps to set the flower onto the side of the cake, but can be cut off if the flower is to be set flat.

Wedge pea

I couldn't resist the colours of this lovely relation of the sweet pea. The size and shape of the flowers are much the same but the front crescent is placed differently.

Method

1. Make a 60mm long crescent of white paste and insert the hooked end of a piece of wire into it.
2. Make a Dainty Bess type petal the size of a one cent coin and hollow it out slightly from the back.
3. Moisten petal and attach to the back of the crescent. Make sure petal stands up well.
4. Curve the end of the crescent forward and slightly downward leaving the petal standing up and away from it.

5. Colour the crescent half way up the back petal with lipstick-pink powdered chalk.
6. Colour rest of petal with yellow chalk.

7. Colour the edges of the back petal with the pink chalk.

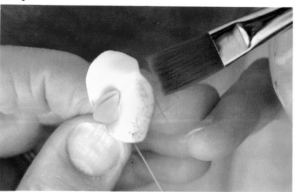

8. Roll two very tiny balls of paste, moisten and attach one at each side of the bottom of the crescent at the front. Allow to dry then colour them a bright yellow. They look like two small eyes.

Sturt's desert pea

*T*his striking flower adds that extra something to a spray of native flowers. Be careful to keep the size in proportion to that of the other flowers in the spray.

Method

1. Make a crescent-shaped petal approximately 2.5cm long and curve the tail forwards and upwards.

2. Make two small tear-drops of paste 60mm long and fold the long edges towards each other to form an ear.
3. Moisten and attach on each side of the front of the top of the crescent.
4. Shape the ends of all three petals together and to a point. Allow to dry.
5. Make a small ball of paste and attach it to the point with a dab of paste glue (paste dissolved in water until it becomes mushy).
6. If you wire the flower, insert the hooked wire into the ball now. Allow to dry.
7. Make a petal from a small triangle of paste, with a rounded base.
8. Flute the straight edges.
9. Place petal in the palm of your left hand and hollow out the centre of the rounded base.
10. Lightly wet the underside of the petal and place across the top of the three joined petals just where the ball is attached. Quickly lift it up toward, over and around the ball to make a 'bulge' then ease the rest of the petal backward so that it stands up well. Look at the photographs to see exactly how you do this tricky bit. Allow to dry.

11. Apart from the 'bulge' paint the flower scarlet. Bring the paint to the edges of the petals and close up to the underside of the bulge. Allow to dry.
12. Mix a little black and purple paint and paint the 'bulge' feathering the colour out in to the scarlet.

Gum nuts

*T*he light-brown colour gives the right touch to a spray of native flowers.

Method

1. Make a small dumpy cone of nut-brown modelling paste and open it up with the small ball-tool till it is as wide across the top of the cone as it is long. Wire and allow to dry.
2. Roll out a small piece of paste which will fill the hollow in the cone. Dampen it and fit it into place. Make a cross on the flat top.
3. Paint some nuts a darker brown and some green.

Gum blossom

*T*hese unusual flowers are made from threads of brightly-coloured red, orange or yellow sewing cotton set in dark-brown or dark-green gum nuts. They soften a spray of other native flowers.

Flower

1. Hold your left thumb and forefinger 1.25cm apart and, leaving a tail of cotton hanging, wind cotton around them 20 times.

2. Take the cotton off your fingers, tie the tail round the centre of the loop to make a figure-8 and tie off. Bind the centre of the loop with fine wire leaving a long end.

3. Fold the figure-8 in half so that all the loops face in the same direction and bind the wire round it so that all the loops are standing up at the end of the wire stem.

4. Cut the top of the loops open.

5. Make a gum nut from brown or green paste, pass the bottom of the wire through it, and push the nut up to fit neatly round the flower and neaten on to the wire. Leave to dry.

6. Separate the threads. Touch the tips lightly with a little glue made by dissolving scraps of modelling glue in water till they become mushy and dip them in some powdered gelatine mixed with either green or yellow powdered chalk. Only a speck on each thread is needed — don't make the tips lumpy.

Leaf

The leaf is long and thin, tapering to a point at the top with one central vein. Three flowers and three leaves are used to make a spray.

Tea-tree

The pretty mauve-pink colour of the flowers and the dark green of the leaves makes the tea-tree very useful as a filler for a spray of native flowers.

Flower

1. Hollow out a small cone of white modelling paste with a round-headed toothpick.

2. Make five short cuts into the rim to create five petals.

3. Gently smooth away the curves of each petal.
4. Flatten each one, pushing the paste sideways.
5. Indent the centre with the small ball tool. Allow flower to dry.
6. Mix burgundy-pink and mauve-pink colours with a little pure alcohol. Paint the back of the petals — then paint the front. Allow to dry.

7. Fill the hollow centre of the flower with royal icing and bring it up to a peak. Allow to dry.
8. Paint the centre a blackish-green.

Leaves

Neaten a long bean of paste on to a knotted wire and flatten to make a long spindly leaf. Paint dark green.

Flannel flowers

*T*hese are certainly one of the prettiest native flowers but also one of the hardest to make. I have tried all ways, cutting it like a daisy, working on a ring, petal for petal and assembling when dry, but I found the best method is to make and dry the centre and then place the wet petals on to it. You must work very quickly however, and of course, work in white paste.

Centre method

1. Wire a ball of fondant about the size of a 1 cent coin, any bigger and the flower will be out of proportion to the waratah which it usually accompanies in a spray. Allow to dry.

2. Mix together some dry-powdered gelatine and finely dusted moss-green chalk and place in a container.
3. Paint the top half of the dried centre with green colouring and while still damp dip it into the dry mixture. Allow to dry.

Flower method

1. Make five or six finely pointed petals which widen in the middle and narrow towards the bottom.

2. Fit the damp petals around the centre and make firm.

3. Make another four or five petals and fit these behind the first ones, filling in the spaces. Allow to dry.

4. Paint the back of the petals a pale-yellow colour mixed with pure alcohol.
5. Touch the tip of each petal with glue made by dissolving a few scraps of modelling paste in water until they become misty then dip them in the gelatine and chalk mixture used for the centre.

Geraldton wax and Esperance

*B*oth these flowers take their names from the areas in which they grow in Western Australia. They make very effective fillers for a spray of native flowers. Geraldton wax is pink with a deeper pink centre, Esperance is snow white with a sharp lime-green centre.

Method

1. Hollow out a 1.25cm core of white modelling paste with a round toothpick.
2. Make five short cuts in the rim to create five petals.
3. Trim the corners of each petal very slightly.

4. Place the open blades of paint scissors round the petals at the bottom and squeeze gently.

5. Flatten each petal and cup each one using a small ball-tool.

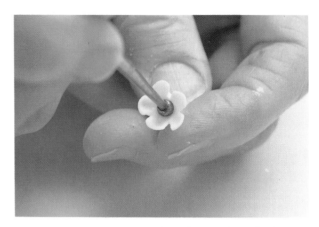

6. Indent the centre of each petal with the ball-tool. Cut away the paste at the back of the flower so that it can dry flat.
7. Wire a very small gum nut shape, fill it with royal icing, and set the flower in it. Allow to dry.
8. Using a very fine pipe, pipe a dot of royal icing at the base of each petal on the edge of the indented centre. Then pipe a long, pulled dot in the centre of it.
9. Paint the back of the Geraldton wax flower pink-mauve. When dry, paint the centre in a darker shade of the same colour. Mix the colour with pure alcohol.
10. Esperance is pure white. Paint the centre a sharp lime green (moss green with a touch of yellow) and pull up a dot of lime-green royal icing at the base of each petal around the indented area.

Christmas bush

*T*he pink 'flowers' left on the bush when the white flowers are over are actually the calyx. They enlarge and gradually turn to the colour which gives the bush its name. As it is not a true red, you will have to mix paint carefully.

Flower method

1. Hollow out a tiny core of white modelling paste with a round-headed toothpick.
2. Make five long cuts of equal depth and equally spaced apart to create five petals.

3. Mitre each petal, cupping the centre of each one very slightly.
4. Flatten and shape upwards.
5. Wire the flower, re-cupping the centre and neatening the back on to the wire. Make some flowers with half-closed petals to give variety.

6. Paint the centre of each flower yellow. Allow to dry.

7. Mix rose-pink paint with a touch of orange in pure alcohol and paint the back of each petal. Paint the front of each petal from the centre of the flower outwards leaving a small margin of white around the yellow centre.

Buds

Shape a small piece of white modelling paste on to the end of a knotted piece of wire to make a long slender bud. Paint the bud pink with a little yellow showing at the tip.

Leaves

The leaves are made up of three small leaflets with finely serrated edges, rather like a maple-leaf.

Five flowers and four buds are assembled to make a cluster used as a filler. Wire each flower and bud separately and bind the wires together with pale-green tissue paper or Stemtex. Do not use Parafilm; it is too heavy.

Decorating sides

Extension

A skirt border decoration around the base of a cake of finely piped threads of royal icing extending to a scalloped edge along the bottom is called extension. It is also referred to as bridgework, dropwork or threadwork.

The scalloped edge is the extension and the threadwork of the skirt is the bridgework or dropwork.

If you are a beginner develop your skills by practising on the side of a cake tin before working on a cake.

1. Measure the length and height of one side of the cake and cut a piece of greaseproof paper to this size for a template. (If it is a round cake cut the paper long enough to encircle the cake.

2. Fold the paper in half crosswise. Cut a half scallop at the cut ends of the template. The half scallop at the corner of the cake will meet the half from the adjoining side and avoid an ugly finish at each corner of the cake.

3. With the template folded in half, fold again up to the beginning of the half scallop and continue until the desired scallop size is obtained. Cut a shallow curve through all thicknesses of the template to create the scallop pattern. When you open the template there will be half a scallop pattern at each end.

4. Fold the template in half crosswise and fold lengthwise to form the top design of the extension. The fold can be a straight line 3cm above the scallop line or the line can be lower at the ends meeting at a centre position 3cm above the scallop line or any variation which pleases you. This line marks the position from which the threadwork drops down to the extended scallops.

5. Pipe a small snail's trail around the base of the cake to fasten it to the board.

6. Pin each end of the template onto the side of the cake making sure that the scallops just touch the snail's trail. If the scallops are any lower they will fasten to the board and break when the cake is moved. On the other hand, if the edge is too high the skirt will not cover the bottom neatly.

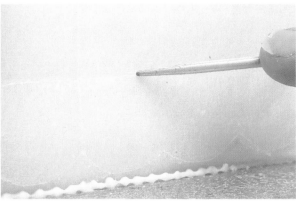

7. Using the blunt end of a No. 10 knitting needle trace the design over the paper template onto the cake. Repeat on all sides being sure to match up the corner scallops.

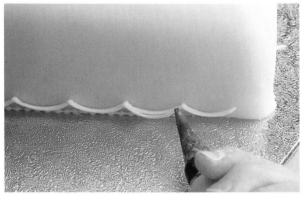

8. Using a No. 2 tube, pipe a row of royal icing over the scallop design. When the row is thoroughly dry, pipe another row over the first. Repeat this 6 times. Make sure the rows are evenly extended from each other.

9. After the dropwork is dry (it may take a few hours) use a No. 00 tube, a new batch of royal icing and attach the threadwork. Holding the tube firmly and using even pressure start from the top design line and draw the thread down and out onto the built out scallop design. Continue to add the threadwork being careful to watch that: —
   - the space between each thread is close and equal;
   - the tension of each thread is the same.

10. Once the threadwork is dry finish the bottom edge with scallops, tiny loops, a fine rope design or dots. The top edge can be finished by applying lace pieces or tiny loops and dots.

Cutter designs

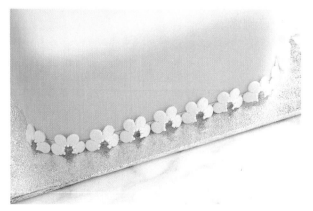

Commercial cutters are available in numerous designs and can be used individually or to build a design using fondant. In the illustration I have used flower cutters.

1. From a 3mm thick rolled fondant sheet cut out a flower and remove the two lower petals.
2. Using a small daisy-design cutter remove the centre from the flower.
3. Curve the design into a shallow U-shape and place to dry.
4. Attach to the side of the cake with royal icing.

Some designs when attached over a ribbon allow the ribbon to show through the centre cutout.

Frill

*T*he original frill is the Garrett Frill from South Africa. It can be placed around the cake or up and over the side of the cake. A Garrett Frill cutter enables you to make this decoration easily.

1. Roll fondant to 3mm thick. Cut with the Garrett Frill cutter.

2. Cut the design in half. Press with a rounded toothpick and fan out each scallop until it starts to frill.

3. Trim the top edge to an even width and attach to the cake with egg-white and water.
4. Finish the top with a ease edging or the imprint of a small cutter.

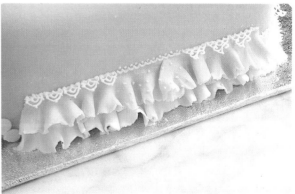

Marzipan fruit

Marzipan fruits are made from the almond paste used to cover cakes; you can make the marzipan yourself or buy it ready-made. The fruits make a very pretty addition to a cake or, if presented attractively in a small box, a pleasant little gift. You can make apples, pears, strawberries, bananas, cherries, oranges, grapes, etc, so that you have a lovely assortment of colours.

Just mould the fruit from a small ball of marzipan and leave to dry with a clove in the top as a stalk and another in the bottom. Paint when the paste is dry. You can make vegetables in the same way.

To make a fruit barrel

I make fruit barrels in which to present the fruit. The top of a Tupperware egg-cup makes just the right-sized mould.

1. Cornflour the egg-cup well. Roll out a little white modelling paste and fit it into the egg-cup, working out the thickness and shaping it to fit and make a neat barrel shape.
2. Trim the top edge and gently take the little barrel out of the egg-cup. Redust the cup with cornflour and put the barrel back into it to dry.
3. Paint it brown.
4. Make tiny twisted 'ropes' to go around the top and bottom of the barrel. Attach with a little water and leave to dry.
5. Paint the twists a darker brown than the barrel.

Floodwork

There are endless ways of using this type of cake decoration and many different types of design can be used. What you are actually doing is reproducing an existing design in royal icing. Cards and pictures can be used as models. I find this medium particularly useful when one is decorating a cake for a man. His hobbies, sporting interests and work can all be portrayed in a bold and interesting way.

These are the three ways of doing floodwork. The first one described is the traditional way.

Materials needed

A card or picture, preferably in colour, of the design you wish to reproduce. (The work will be made easier if you have two copies of the design.) Uncreased wax paper, sticky-tape, pencil, royal icing, 00 tube, lemon juice, 30cm board.

Method 1 — traditional

1. Sticky-tape the design to the board. Do not allow the tape to touch any part of the design.
2. Cover the design with waxed paper, waxy side uppermost and sticky-tape it down.
3. Using a lead pencil outline the design,

visible through the waxpaper, on to the paper.

4. Using royal icing of piping consistency, follow the design. Allow to dry.

5. Pipe a second row of icing on top of the first outline.

6. To fill in the areas within the outlines, use royal icing mixed with lemon juice — the flatter and smoother the texture of the design, the more lemon juice is needed. You can use white royal icing and colour it when dry or colour the icing before use. If you only have a small area to cover, it is simpler to use white icing and paint it later. Black areas should always be of white royal icing painted, when dry, with colour straight from the bottle. Using a paint brush and palette knife, fill in and cover the outline. Use the icing either smooth or rough depending on the design, eg, eyes are smooth and round, Father Christmas's beard is thick and fluffy. Always allow one colour to dry before applying the next otherwise the stronger colour will bleed into the paler one.

7. When you have completed the filling in — the flooding — remove the design and use it as a copy to paint in the fine detail. This is where a second copy of the design can come in useful.

Note
Always use a pale colour to flood in an animal shape and hair too, whether it is dark or fair. The colour can be adjusted with paint later. Use red-powdered flood colouring for a Christmas red and always mix it well.

Remember that you are actually creating a three-dimensional plaque, so contour any human bodies in the design, give the face a nose (apply with several coats), eye-brows, moustache, etc, using royal icing.

Method 2 — run-in floodwork

1. Trace your design on to greaseproof paper.

2. Turn the paper over, place it in a dry modelling paste plaque and retrace the design so that it is outlined on the plaque.

3. Choose the colours you need and mix some of each with royal icing and a little water and keep covered.

4. Start to flood-in the design beginning with the area furthest away. Let each area dry before proceeding to the next and work your way to the front of the design. Leave to dry.

5. Paint in the details using the original design as a copy. You can paint in grass and flowers and use small moulded or piped flowers to enhance the picture.

Method 3 — moulded work

You will need good moulds but this is certainly the quickest way. For a Father Christmas face:

1. Dust the inside of the mould with cornflour and press rolled-out white modelling paste onto it following the contours of the mould. Remove excess paste.

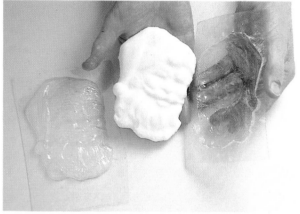

2. Take the face out, redust the mould with cornflour and put it back again. Allow to dry.

3. Using royal icing pipe in the details of the beard and cap then paint the features of the face.

Bootees

*T*his is a different method, thought of by one of my students, and can be used as a decoration for a christening cake.

There are three pieces in the pattern — the sole, the toe and heel.

Method

1. Cut out two soles in white or coloured

paste and dry flat. Do not make them bigger than the pattern. You can make them smaller.

2. Cut out two toes. Dampen the edges and fit around the front part of the sole, shaping the toe up and over as you go.

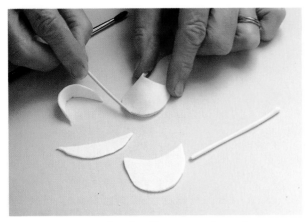

3. Cut out two heels. Dampen the edges and fit around the back part of the sole. Allow shoes to dry.

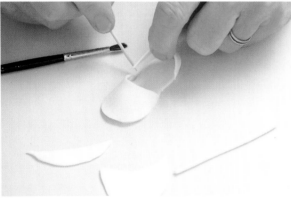

4. Make a flat strap, or roll some paste to make a shoe strap. Attach to the heel so it looks ready to be either buttoned or tied. Attach a pearl stamen to make the button.
5. Use paint mixed with a little pure alcohol if you wish to colour the paste. You can decorate the bootees with scattered forget-me-nots for a girl, or groups of dots for a boy or put a tiny bow at the centre of the toe arch.

Bible or book

A bible or prayer-book and some flowers make a very pretty decoration for the top of a wedding cake. The directions given are for the top of a cake, a smaller version would be suitable for the centre of a bottom tier.

If you are making a Communion cake use the prayer-book and add some rosary beads. If you want a plain bible, the covering must be done very well. The one in the photograph was imprinted with guipure lace and embroidered with royal icing.

Method

1. Cut out a block of modelling paste 7.5cm x 7cm thick.

2. Trim 1.25cm off the longer side and make into a roll.
3. Attach the roll back to the block so that it looks like the curved back of a book.
4. Roll out a rectangle of paste 11.25cm x 7.5cm.

5. Place some guipure lace on the paste and gently make its imprint in the paste. Peel away.
6. Lift up the paste (design outwards) and wrap it around the rectangle of paste, starting at one edge, curling round the roll

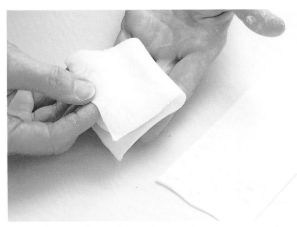

at the back and finishing at the other edge.

7. Mark the length of the book to define where the paste covers the roll so that you have a clearly defined back of the book. Make three horizontal cuts across the roll to delegate space for title, author, etc.

8. Using a sharp knife mark the open end of the book to simulate the paper pages.

9. Fill in the pattern of the lace with piped royal icing.

10. Attach a 7.5cm length of 60mm ribbon as a bookmark.

Bibs

A bib is quick and easy to make. It can be the only decoration used on a 20cm christening cake for a boy or girl. Make it in coloured paste if you wish or in white paste and spray colour it later.

Method 1

1. Using the pattern, cut out the bib in cardboard.

2. Place pattern on rolled-out paste and cut out. Be certain not to drag or tear the paste — if you do you will alter the shape.

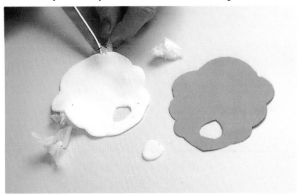

3. Decorate the edges. You can do this *either* by using a tool for making designs on leather *or* by using the top of a teaspoon

handle which has a pretty design or you can leave it plain and decorate it with royal icing later. Tuck a small wad of wax paper under two or three of the shaped patterns to flute up the edges and create a 'flowing' effect.

4. When completely dry decorate the whole bib. You can write *baby* or the child's name and work a design around the letter.

Method 2

1. Make two bibs — the same shape but smaller than the pattern. One will lie on top of the other. The paste of the bottom one is much thicker than that of the top one.
2. Decorate the edges of the upper bib and 'flute up' the edges.
3. Place on top of the thicker bib and join together around the neck with piped royal icing.
4. Tuck a small spray of tiny flowers, to emerge from between the bibs and finish them off with a tiny bow of ribbon.

Knitted bootees

*T*he idea for these came from a knitting book. All the work is done in royal icing of petal consistency. Do follow the pattern carefully. You can use white or coloured modelling paste.

Method

1. Cut two pattern shapes from modelling paste 3.75 cm long and 2.5cm thick.
2. Poke two holes in the bottom of each one to enable the paste to dry out without splitting.

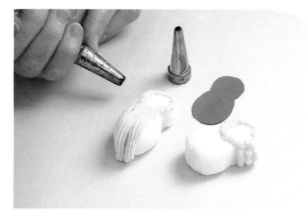

3. With a No. 8 star tube and icing the same colour as the paste, pipe a row of stars around the ankle using a pull-push movement.
4. From the ankle, pipe three flat lines about 1cm long out towards the toe.
5. With the No. 8 star tube pipe vertical lines right round the heel, from one side indent to the other, keeping the lines so close together that no paste can show through.
6. By now, the first row of stars around the ankle will be dry. Pipe a second row of stars on top of it. Leave to dry. Pipe a third row. leave to dry. Pipe a fourth. Leave to dry.
7. Using a No. 12 star tube and holding the bootee up, start in the middle and at the edge of the flat area of the toe and pipe a stroke right over the toe to the sole. Continue making the strokes until the front half of the bootee is completely covered and no paste shows through.
8. Pipe a half circle in a contrasting colour in the toe area between the two lots of piping, using a push-pull action.
9. Using the contrasting colour pipe a fifth row of stars around the ankle.
10. Decorate bootee with a tiny bow.
11. Make another bootee to match.

Christmas crackers

Method

1. Make a cylinder of modelling paste (colour can be whatever you wish) 2.5cm long and 9mm thick. Make a hole in each end so that it can dry out thoroughly.
2. Roll out an oblong piece of paste three times the length of the cylinder and wide enough to encircle it with an overlap.
3. Mark each of the short ends with a pattern to be painted in later. Turn paste over.
4. Place the cylinder of paste in the middle of the oblong piece and gently roll the paste over the middle cylinder to enclose it in a long outer cylinder.
5. Squeeze the outer cylinder very gently at each end of the enclosed cylinder to make the typical 'cracker' shape.
6. Put your left forefinger down into the narrowed shape at one end and your right one down the other one and push together very, very gently.
7. Paint the marked in pattern. Attach stars, cut-out flowers, or any other suitable decoration to the 'barrel' of the cracker.

Fireplace

*T*his is something different for a Christmas cake. I made up my first one as I went along but this one I copied from a card. You could make up your own design quite easily.

Method

1. Cut an oblong piece of paste 10cm thick and of an appropriate size. You can use white modelling paste and paint it later, or a coloured paste — terracotta for bricks — soft yellow for slate.
2. Cut out a half-circle arch low down in the centre front of the block but do not cut through to the back of the paste. You can mark the paste with a scalpel to show the bricks or stones or leave it plain. Dry flat.
3. You can, if you wish, make an arch to outline the arch of the fireplace and mark it to look like bricks or stone. Keep the paste at the same thickness.
4. Make the mantlepiece from a sausage of same thickness, paste flattened. Place it along the top of the fireplace to form the 'mantle shelf'.

How much decoration or variation you add now is entirely up to you. You can paint in a fire-basket, coal and flames, or mould a vase of flowers for the mantlepiece, a coal bucket or a copper hood for the fireplace. Don't forget the holly and berries for the festive touch.

Wishing well

*T*his pretty ornament can be used in a birthday cake. It is only small so will need some flowers as an accompaniment. You will need a very small English jam jar and an empty glass phial like the ones used to contain glitter-dust some toothpicks and a matchbox bottom.

Well method

1. Roll out a ball of paste till it is the size of a 50 cent coin and 1.25cm thick.

2. Cornflour the rim of the jam jar and use it to cut out a circle of paste. Make certain the cut is clean.

3. Using the phial cut a hole in the centre of the paste. Remove the surplus paste.

4. Using a scalpel mark in brickwork all around the circle of paste.
5. Insert one toothpick in the top of the rim of the paste and then another one directly opposite it. These will hold the roof of the well in position. Keep turning the toothpicks to prevent them from sticking to the paste as it dries. You will need to be able to remove them at will. Leave the well to dry.

Roof method

1. Roll out a piece of paste till it is 5cm x 7.5cm and 30mm thick.
2. Mark in the slats using a scalpel. Start at the edge of the long sides and work inwards leaving a blank space in the centre where the capping will be.
3. Fit the roof into the matchbox bottom, marked side downwards. Place one side along the bottom of the box and gently bend the paste so that it stands upright against the side. Support it with a ball of cotton wool. Allow to dry.

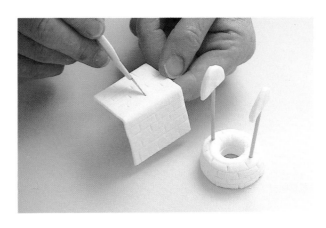

Side structure method

1. Use pattern and cut two from paste 60mm thick. Insert a toothpick in each one leaving enough protruding to fit into the holes in the well-base. Place flat and leave to dry.

Now paint the well and the roof and leave to dry.

To assemble

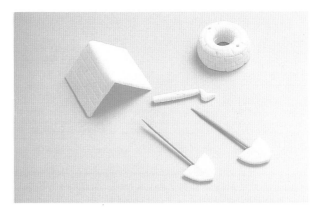

1. Position the side structures in the holes making sure the tops are level. Secure with royal icing.

2. Attach the roof using royal icing. Leave to dry.
3. Roll a tiny piece of white paste thinly long enough to reach each toothpick. Attach the ends to the toothpicks with royal icing. This is the piece of wood to which the bucket and rope are attached. Leave to dry.
4. Pipe rope around the 'piece of wood' leaving an end which can be attached to a bucket.
5. Decorate the well with vines and flowers — moulded or piped.

Bells

A bell for a wedding cake is long and slender, a Christmas bell is wider and more solid-looking and has a shoulder. You can buy the moulds in either plastic, glass or brass.

You can mould the bell by fitting paste around the outside of it and making a neat join, or by shaping the paste round the inside of the bell, in which case you have no join, but you will have more difficulty in making the paste thin enough and still able to hold the shape.

Method

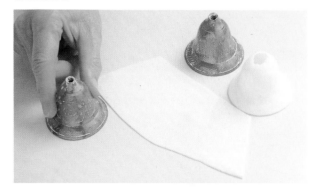

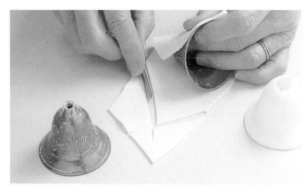

1. Cornflour the outside of the mould.
2. Roll out paste thinly and cut into a rough
   bell shape.

3. Fold around the mould until the sides
   meet. Take off paste mould and trim away
   excess paste.

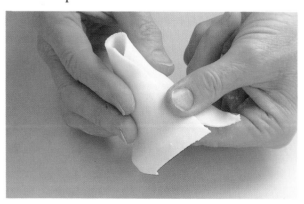

4. Re-cornflour the mould, replace the bell.
   Dampen paste at edge of join and smooth
   to make the join as invisible as possible.

5. Ease the paste at both top and bottom of
   the bell and cut away the excess.
6. Take paste off mould again and re-
   cornflour to make certain they cannot
   stick together. Make your final shaping.

7. While paste is still damp you can use tiny flower-cutters to cut out shapes on the bell. Make sure cuts are clean. Leave to dry on mould.

8. Dust the inside with cornflour and decorate the outside with cornelli (see royal icing) or a pattern of dots. If the join is less than perfect, hide it with tiny flowers or any other small decoration. To make an edging around the bottom of the bell, mark it into sixteenths with a spot of royal icing and pipe loops of royal icing between the dots. Allow to dry then pipe another layer of icing drops on top of the first one. Allow to dry. Do this twice more so that the piping stands out from the bell. Join the edging to the bell with fine threadwork. Finish with a snail trail and a tiny loop edging. Place a tiny forget-me-not with a coloured stamen head between the scalloped loops of icing around the bell.

9. Close up the top of the bell with royal icing.

10. If the bells are less than 7.5cm in size, use two. Fill the bells with small filler flowers, ribbon and ribbon loops. Place them side by side on their sides with a tiny spray of filler flowers between them and loops of ribbon up and behind them.

Slippers

*T*his same method can be used to make bootees, ballet shoes, football boots, etc. Don't make them too big, because they become hard to mould and match.

Method

1. Roll a sausage of modelling fondant 7½cm long and 4cm in diameter.
2. Flatten along the top.
3. Cut the block into two, match in length and height. Round the toe area.
4. Take a round-ended piece of dowel 2cm in diameter and push it into the block from half-way down to the toe area.
5. Mould the toe area over this and pull up the tongue.
6. Now reverse the dowel towards the heel section and work out the foot area.
7. Smooth out the inside of the slipper.
8. Colour by painting with straight colour and trim with a royal icing frilled shell to represent feet.

Chocolate

*T*his is a fun area of cake decorating. You can use pure chocolate or compound chocolate and it is very important to understand the difference. Pure chocolate must be at exactly the right temperature while you are working with it otherwise it will stick to the mould and turn white as it dries, because the cocoa butter in the mixture has separated. Compound chocolate will not do this. The cocoa butter has been extracted and oil has replaced it and this allows it to come out of the mould easily.

Compound chocolate is not as smooth as the real thing but I have found that if I mix 500g of it with a family size block of dairy milk chocolate the mixture works very well and has a lovely taste. You can make moulded choclates, flowers, leaves and, of course, Easter eggs.

Easter eggs

You can buy plastic moulds with which to make the eggs.

Fill one half of the mould with hot melted chocolate. Clip on the other half of the mould, matching the edges carefully so that the chocolate will not spurt out. Twist the closed mould round and round so that the chocolate will coat the whole of the inside of the mould as evenly as possible. Put it into the refrigerator and leave until it is really cold. When you open the mould the chocolate egg should lift out easily.

Leaves

The photographs show leaves made in a mould, and by painting liquid chocolate on to a real leaf. When the chocolate sets it can be easily lifted from the leaf.

The other photograph shows what happens when fillings are dipped into chocolate which is too hot.

Chocolate for piping

Add one or two drops of glycerine to 60g melted compound chocolate to thicken the chocolate and make it suitable for using to make lace, scrolls, lattice-work and writing. Use a paper cornet bag with the end cut to make the required size opening and to work more quickly than you would if you were using royal icing as the chocolate hardens more quickly. If the choclate becomes too hard to use you will have to empty it out of the bag, remix it and start again with a new bag.

Chocolate for moulding

Add 15g warmed glucose and 15g corn syrup to 60g melted compound chocolate. Mix thoroughly. Wrap in clingwrap and leave in the refrigerator for about an hour before you use it.

Pink oval birthday cake

$\mathcal{T}$his small oval cake can be made very quickly. The plaque is cocoa-painted.

To make the plaque

1. Cut out the shape of the plaque in modelling paste and leave to dry thoroughly. Keep turning it over for a few days until you are sure both sides are bone dry.
2. Trace your chosen design on to greaseproof paper. Turn it over and pencil the design on

the back. Turn it back again and trace the design on to the dry plaque as lightly but as legibly as possible.

3. Melt a dessertspoon of cocoa butter (obtainable from a chemist) in a small container over hot water and add a little cocoa powder. Do not mix it all in. Keep some of it paler, for the light parts of the design and then mix in more cocoa powder for the darker areas. Paint in the design using the lighter and darker butter as needed.

4. Allow the painted plaque to dry. Be sure not to touch any of the painted parts with your fingers.

This is one of the easiest ways of decorating a small cake and some very pretty effects can be created.

Boy's christening cake

*B*aby-blue fondant covers the cake and teddy bears are the theme. The little ones on the top were made from modelling paste with piped royal icing for the fur. I painted them when they were dry. You could make the bears from marzipan instead. The nylon ribbon was dyed with brown paint mixed with pure alcohol to match the colour of the bears; the tiny flower sprays are primulas and bluebells.

To make teddy bears

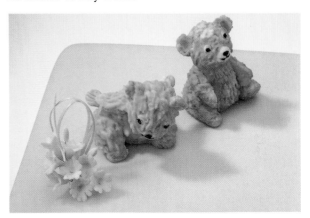

1. Mould a pear-shaped piece of modelling paste to make the body of the bear and insert a round toothpick into the neck, leaving enough protruding to take the head.
2. Make the arms and legs from little sausages of paste, nipping them in to make the wrists and ankles and flattening the ends to make the paws and feet.
3. Attach to the body with a little water.

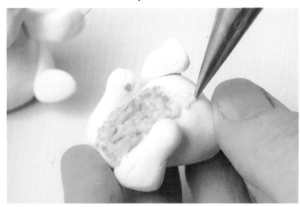

4. Make the head from a much smaller pear-shaped piece of paste, shaping the nose and making little indentations for the eyes.

Mould two little ears. Make a slit on each side of the head and fit the ears into them.
5. Make a couple of holes in the underside of the body so the paste can dry evenly and leave for a good time to make certain the body is dry all the way through.

6. Using royal icing, pipe short downward strokes all over the bear to make the fur.
7. Fill in the eye indentations with a little paste.
8. When completely dry, paint the bear a light caramel, brown and paint in the detail of the eyes, nose and mouth.

Daphne cake

*T*his pretty cake is suitable for a birthday, anniversary or an engagement. Instructions for making the flowers are in the Moulded Flower section. You can use embroidery of your own design for the side decoration but be sure to use a template so that you can keep it regular.

Girl's christening cake

The frill is made by using an eight-petal daisy cutter. Make the modelling paste as fine as possible. Roll the petals with a toothpick and leave to dry on a curved surface. There are six pattern pieces for the cradle.

Method

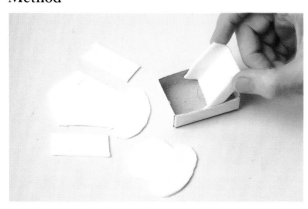

1. From white modelling paste cut out pattern pieces 1, 2 and 3. Cut out two of piece 4.
2. Dry 1, 2 and 4 flat.
3. While paste is damp turn up both sides of piece 3 about 1cm and support while it dries. This is the bed part of the cradle.

4. Attach the ends of 3 to the bottom half of 1 with a thread of royal icing. Allow to dry.
5. Attach piece 2 to the other end of piece 3 in the same way. Make sure the cradle is level and will rock. Allow to dry.

6. Attach both side pieces, 4 and allow to dry.

7. Lie the cradle on its back, cut out piece

5 and while still damp mould it around the top and join to the side pieces. Allow to dry.

8. Mix brown paint with pure alcohol and paint the cradle to create the effect of wood.

9. Mould a baby, pillow and cover.
   Pillow: Mould from a ball of fondant; round both ends and half flatten.
   Cover: Roll a thin, 5cm square, piece of fondant. Mark the small squares with the back of a knife.
   While wet place in cradle.
   When dry paint squares.

10. Decorate cradle with a garland of tiny flowers of mixed colour.

Girl's birthday cake

I wanted something a bit different for this one. I made the colour by mixing caramel with a *little* green and chestnut-brown. The beads and bangles and earrings are all made from white modelling paste and were painted when the paste was dry. I used bouvandia and primroses as the flower decoration around the base of the cake.

To make the bangles

1. Roll out a ball of modelling paste 2.5cm in diameter. Using the rim of a small jam-jar cut into a neat circle.

2. Using a smaller jar as a cutter (I used a pill phial) cut out the centre of the paste and gently lift it out and discard it.

3. Mould the circle of paste left with your fingers to make a bangle and paint it when dry.

Train

*J*am rolls and rollettes, liquorice, chocolate biscuits, buttercream and plenty of colourful lollies are used to make the train. Just follow the photograph.

Buttercream recipe

> *75-125g softened butter*
> *200-250g pure icing sugar*
> *2 teaspoons lemon juice*
> *liquid food colouring*
> *25g cocoa powder (optional)*
> *sweet sherry to taste (optional)*

Method

Beat the butter in an electric mixer on medium speed, adding a dessertspoon of icing sugar at a time till it is all light and fluffy. Mix in lemon juice. Colour with liquid food colouring. If you do not use this at once it must be kept in the refrigerator. It must be brought out 12 hours before you wish to use it to allow it to regain room temperature.

By adding 25g cocoa powder and some sweet sherry you can turn the buttercream mixture into Vienna cream.

Dolly Varden cake for a little girl

Quick version

Make a simple butter cake in a Dolly Varden tin and allow to cool. You now need a 9cm doll, with legs, and with or without hair. Push the doll up to the waist into the centre of the cake so that the cake becomes its skirt. Decorating is now up to you.

You can use different sized star tubes and buttercream to pipe the skirt design and the body of the doll as the top of the dress. You can adorn her head with a little piped icing; tuck a little flower into her hand and surround her with colourful lollies — which will be the most important part of the cake. This is all very quick and simple to do. A bow of ribbon completes the effect.

If you can take more time and trouble you can cover a fruit cake with fondant and decorate it as a nursery rhyme figure, old fashioned-lady, a Dutch girl — the variety is endless — but there will be hours of work involved and the cake will be eaten just as quickly!

Father's day cake

*T*his is a rectangular cake with a card of moulded tools as the theme. The colour is a mixture of sky blue with a touch of mauve. The sides are simple with a shell border and two strands of narrow burgundy-coloured ribbon. Light embroidery depicting sports enhance the Father's day theme.

Method

1. Make the card approximately 12.5cm x 7.5cm x 3mm.
2. Mark in wood-grain with a ruler.
3. Make nail holes while paste is wet.

4. Leave flat to dry, turning over every four hours.
5. When dry, paint with browns and give a wooden wall appearance.

Tools

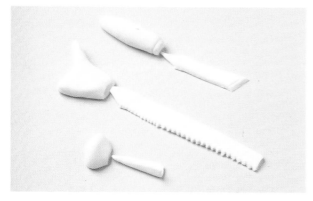

Can be of your own chosing, maybe to represent a particular trade.

1. Mould each one, keeping them in proportion.
2. When dry, paint the handles in a darker brown than the card.
3. Paint all iron parts in silver paint. This is not easy to obtain, but you can buy felt pens which are non-toxic gold and silver in colour.
4. Allow to dry then stick on the card with royal icing. Allow to dry.

Christmas cake

*T*his 20cm square cake covered in white fondant has the poinsettia as the main decoration. A scroll, Christmas rose, holly leaves and cones, shells and a leaf all made from modelling paste add to the pattern. The side design was piped from a bag of royal icing which had a streak of red and green down the sides so that the icing is variegated in the Christmas colours. Thin red ribbon adds the finishing touch.

To make a poinsettia

1. Make twenty 2.5cm long beans of red modelling paste and shape them to a longish point at each end.

2. Flatten them and widen them in the middle.
3. Draw in veins with the back of the knife. They are leaves not flowers.
4. You need 10 tiny green paste gum nuts for the centre of each poinsettia. Make these by pushing a ball-tool into a tiny cone of paste. Leave them all to dry.
5. Pat a dob of royal icing in the centre of a square of waxed paper.
6. Make the shape of the poinsettia, using two rows of red leaves, by placing the lower points in the royal icing.
7. Fill the centre of each poinsettia with gum nuts which are themselves filled with royal icing. Leave to dry.
8. Colour the gum nuts a darker green and the icing in them yellow, with a speck of red.

Twenty-first birthday cake for a girl

*T*he fondant covering is a soft lemon yellow and I chose pretty field flowers, with some wheat for the sprays. Two different lace patterns are used in the design with the small symbolic keys for coming-of-age.

To make buttercups

1. Hollow out a 2cm long cone of modelling paste quite widely.
2. Make five long cuts into the rim to make the petals.
3. Mitre the edges of the petals to make them round.

4. Using a large ball-tool roll each petal sideways and lengthwise, cupping them gently.

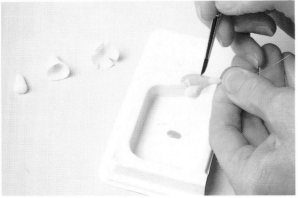

5. Ease the petals so that they overlap and make a cupped flower.
6. Using a tiny dob of royal icing fill the centre with stamen threads.
7. Paint the petals bright yellow with paint straight from the bottle. Tip each stamen thread with brown paint.

To make poppies

1. Make five Dainty Bess petals about 2.5cm long. Flute the top edge gently and leave to dry.
2. Paint the bottom quarter of each petal yellow and leave to dry.

3. Paint the rest of each petal pillar-box red. Allow to dry.
4. Touch the dried yellow part of the petal with a little green colour. Wipe off and touch over with the red colour, just leaving a point of yellow.
5. Shape the five petals into the poppy-shape with a little royal icing, leaving room for the insertion of a moulded centre.
6. Make a very small cone of modelling paste, flatten the top and mark it with a cross.
7. Insert the moulded centre into the petals and surround it with black stamens, using royal icing to keep them all in place.
8. Pipe over the cross with royal icing and, while it is wet, dust it with yellow chalk.

Fortieth anniversary cake

*R*uby-red and white are the colours to use for this anniversary. I chose roses with white flowers as fillers and floodwork for this dramatic number. Frills and tiny loops make the side design.

To make the figured number

1. Trace 4 and 0 on to greaseproof paper. Space them apart.
2. Cover with waxed paper and outline with royal icing, using a 00 tube. Leave to dry.
3. Fill in with royal icing mixed with a little water and brush lightly to make the filling smooth and even. Allow to dry.
4. Paint.
5. When dry, edge the numbers with royal icing dots. Make two dots close together, leave a space then pipe two more all around. When these are dry pipe another dot between each set of two.
6. Lift when safely dry and place on the cake.

One-tier wedding cake

This oval cake is covered in a soft cream fondant. The plaque is run-in floodwork and the flowers around the edges are open roses and tiny pink apple-blossom. The open roses are made from Dainty Bess petals which are painted on the back with a pale-pink colour mixed with pure alcohol. The decoration is completed by four rows of

scallops around the base of the cake with lacework and a tiny apple-blossom in the centre.

To make the apple-blossom

1. Make five of the tiniest Dainty Bess petals you can.

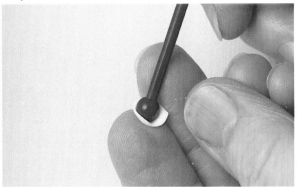

2. Using the ball end of a hair-roller pin, cup each one. Allow to dry.

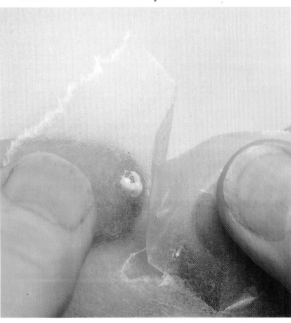

3. Place a very small dob of royal icing in the centre of a cup of waxed paper and arrange

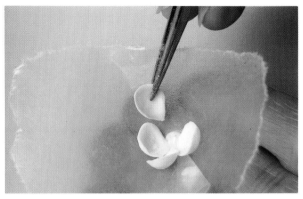

the petals so that they overlap and the last one tucks behind the first one.
4. Insert four or five short stamen threads into the centre of the flower. Allow to dry.
5. Paint the back of the petals with pink colour mixed with alcohol and tip the end of the stamen threads with burgundy paint.

Two-tier octagonal cake

*T*his two-tier octagonal cake features sweetheart rose and eriostemon as fillers. Dainty embroidery on the sides with extension combined with lace inset completes the sides. The ring pillars are different and give an uncluttered look to the tiers.

Eriostemon

1. Make a 60mm cone and hollow out, finely.
2. Cut five long cuts into the rim of the cone to make five petals.

3. Mitre each one into a gentle point and flatten each petal.
4. Wire and cup the petals gently.

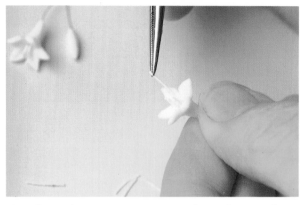

5. Place three short stamen threads into the

centre of the little cupped flower.

Colour

1. When dry, paint only the back of the flower with pink and pure alcohol.
2. Paint the stamen threads and leave to dry thoroughly.
3. Lastly, tip the very top edge of the thread with a speck of brown.

Bells

1. Make and wire a longish bud.
2. Paint when dry with pink and pure alcohol.
3. When dry, paint on a very pale green calyx.

Design of lace inset in pattern pages.

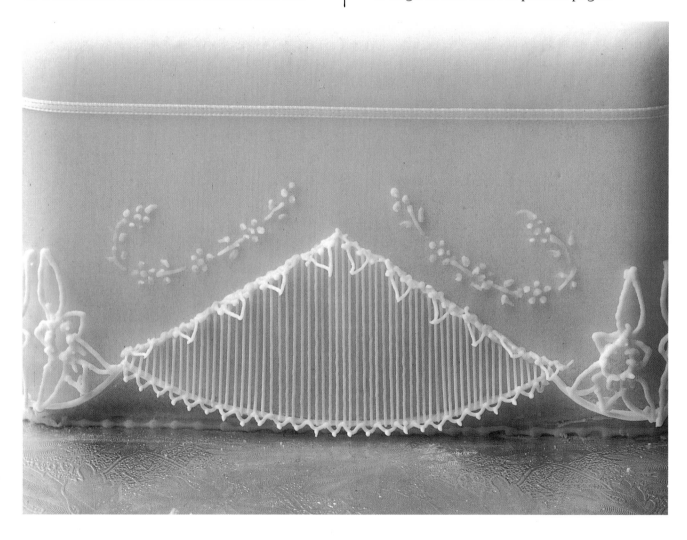

Three-tier wedding cake

*E*ach piece of lace covering the ribbon at the base of this hexagonal-shaped cake is made separately. Make as described for 'lace' and, when dry, lift carefully and place over the ribbon, attaching it carefully with royal icing. The small flowers in the sprays are rosebuds, primulas, hyacinths and bouvardia. A dovecote, surrounded by sprays of the same small flowers decorates the top of the cake.

To make the dovecote

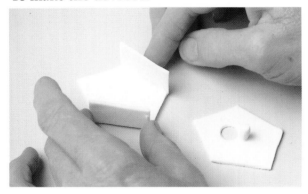

1. Using the pattern, cut one front, one back and two sides of the cote. Dry flat.
2. While the front is still damp cut out a small circle to make the entrance to the cote.
3. Attach the front to the two sides with a little royal icing. Allow to dry.
4. Attach the back to the two sides with a little royal icing. Make sure everything is level and that the cote will stand up safely. Allow to dry.
5. Cut a strip of modelling paste 60mm wider than the roof area with a 60mm overlap at each end.
6. Attach at once with royal icing to the four sides of the cote to make a neat roof. Allow to dry.
7. Make a base of modelling paste 1.25cm larger than the cote base all round. Dry flat.
8. Attach the cote to the base with a little royal icing.
9. Make a tiny perch in modelling paste, and, when dry, attach to the cote just under the hole in the front.

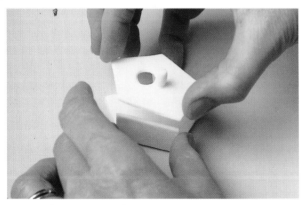

10. Make two small birds. Mould the paste delicately. Put one on the perch and one on the base.

11. Roll out a piece of modelling paste 2.5cm thick and 1.25cm in diameter and allow to dry. This makes a stand for the dovecote. Allow to dry and then attach the whole dovecote to it with royal icing.
12. Decorate the cote with piped royal icing to show the tiles on the roof and any pattern on the walls.

Birthday cake

*T*he avocado colour of the fondant goes well with the golden yellow of the hibbertia which is a very easy flower to make.

Method

1. Mix yellow colouring and a spot of peach colouring into white modelling paste to give the avocado colour.

2. Make a bean of paste 2cm long and pointed at each end. Flatten it and thin out, widening the petal in the middle.
3. Press a small pad of crepe paper in to the petal to give it texture.
4. With a knife make four or five marks down the length of the petal.
5. Finger-flute both sides of the bottom half of the petal.

6. Turn over and roll the top half of each side of the centre vein with a ball-tool. Make five petals for each flower.

To make centre

Take a ball of yellow fondant and half flatten it. This now has a rolled look side view. Now place in half-head stamens about 9cm long making sure you keep the rolled base. Use plenty of stamens to make the centre full. It should be a good 1.25cm in diameter.

Assembly

Place a dob of royal icing on a square of wax paper and place first three petals at 1, 5 and 8 o'clock. Next, overlapping between one and five, place petals number four and number five overlapping between numbers eight and

number seven. Now place the centre in, covering all the royal icing in the centre. Dry in patty tins for support.

Christmas cake

The fondant covering is buff-coloured to highlight the colour of the wild flowers. The koala is in floodwork. I drew the holly leaves for the side decoration, placed waxed paper over the drawings and piped the design using a No. 1 tube for strength, keeping the top edge level. I joined the two leaves together at the top with berries to give support. Carefully lifting leaves and berries attach them to the cake with a little royal icing.

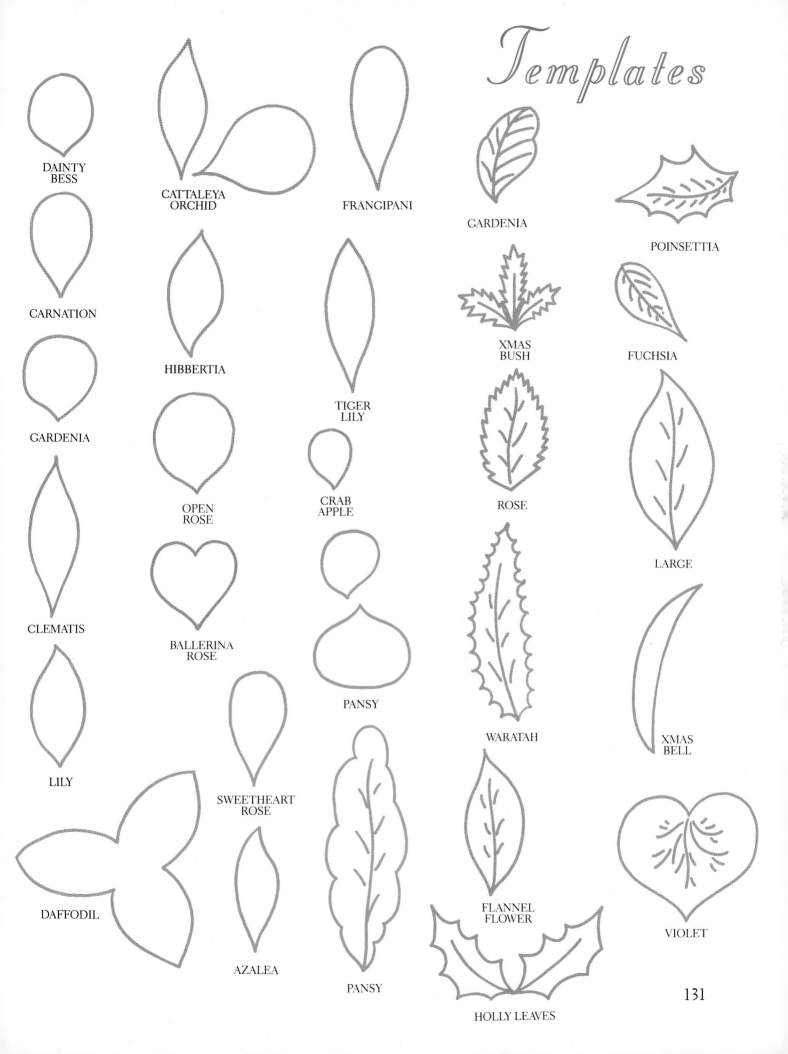

DAINTY
BESS

CATTALEYA
ORCHID

FRANGIPANI

GARDENIA

POINSETTIA

CARNATION

HIBBERTIA

XMAS
BUSH

FUCHSIA

GARDENIA

OPEN
ROSE

CRAB
APPLE

TIGER
LILY

ROSE

LARGE

CLEMATIS

BALLERINA
ROSE

PANSY

WARATAH

XMAS
BELL

LILY

SWEETHEART
ROSE

DAFFODIL

AZALEA

PANSY

FLANNEL
FLOWER

HOLLY LEAVES

VIOLET

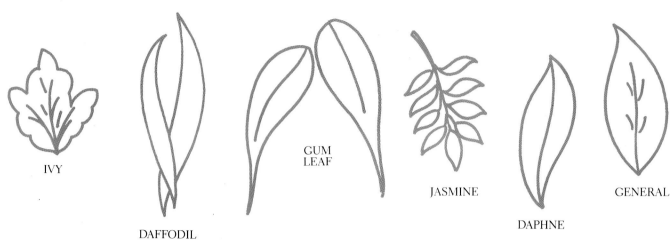

IVY

DAFFODIL

GUM
LEAF

JASMINE

DAPHNE

GENERAL

LACE

PINK OVAL CAKE PLAQUES

CUTTER DESIGN FOR
CHRISTENING CAKE

THREE TIER WEDDING CAKE
DOVE COAT.

TWO TIER WEDDING
CAKE LACE

RING

DAINTY BESS

CRADLE

133

BIBS

BON BON

BIBLE

KNITTED BOOTIE

BOOTIES

BOYS CHRISTENING

GIRLS BIRTHDAY

ONE TIER WEDDING

Index